UNLEASH YOUR BUSINESS ONLINE!

Shubham S. Bapna

For

All the Entrepreneurs, Business Owners, Professionals, and Sales & Marketing Individuals who want to upgrade their Digital Skills and Grand Launch their Digital Journey.

CONTENTS

Preface

After releasing the first edition in 2020, There have been way many changes done in this edition. The crux remains the same, while keeping in mind the errors and updates.

Unleash Your Business Online is the ultimate guide for entrepreneurs and small business owners who want to take their business to the next level.

This book provides easy-to-follow best practices for creating an online presence that will make it easier for customers to find, engage, and purchase from you.

From setting up a website and leveraging social media channels, to understanding the importance of SEO, and optimizing customer experience, this book provides you with strategies, tips, and techniques to help you make the most of the digital space.

Whether you're just starting out or looking to take your business to the next level, Unleash Your Business Online is the ultimate resource for achieving success in the digital age.

Shubham Bapna

Shubham Bapna is a well-known Digital Success Coach, Author, Speaker, and Founder of Grand Launch.

Shubham is currently managing his Businesses across IT, Jewellery, Real Estate, and marketing them both Online and Offline.

The first edition of this book, "Unleash Your Business Online," has also been featured as the Amazon Best Seller.

It's Shubham's mission to simplify Marketing, Sales, and Branding via Grand Launch Academy.

My new Book "Grand Launch" is coming up in 2023.

Foreword

This book is going to be useful for those who are still working traditionally and haven't taken their business online. This is also for those who have expanded digitally, but still facing issuses in making it big. A lot of new ideas to learn- *Sagar Ruparelia, Ofin Legal Private Limited*

Energetic, brainy and out of the box solutions. A lot of positivity makes me to take action now- *Lalit Jain, Advocate, The Legal Desk*

You bring optimism which enhances the creativity to a great extent. I would love to recommend this book not only to entrepreneurs, but also to non-business minds. They are going to love it because of your out of the box thoughts. These make you unique- *Dr. Mittal Jain, Physiotherapist*

This Book can leverage a business in an incremental way. With full of new ideas and enthusiasm, this book is a must read for all- *Dimple Gada, Interior designer*

This Book will open up new horizons for the Ambitious Business Owners. Being an Advocate, I find this book pretty useful and Interesting- *Dhwani Mainkar, Advocate*

There is surely something to learn & implement in my profession too. After reading this book, my mind has started getting highly creative ideas- *Sanjay Doshi, Adinath Print Service*

Acknowledgements

When it comes to thanking and dedicating our genuine work, many people play an essential role. I want to thank my Dad, Mom, Brother, Sister, and my Wife, Dr. Mittal, for their constant support. Doing something this big would have been difficult if they were not around.

I want to thank my Team for their constant support.

I would also like to thank Mr. Arfeen Khan, who gave me a new direction to life and made me aware of my capabilities. I would also like to thank my near and dear ones for their support, always!

Thank you to the Heavenly Powers for guiding me.

Prologue

Unleash Your Business Online is the definitive guide to creating and managing a successful online presence. This book takes readers through the key steps of developing an effective online presence, from creating a strategy and building content to marketing and driving sales.

It provides best practices on how to create an engaging website, how to use SEO, social media, and other digital channels to gain visibility and attract customers, and how to measure and analyze performance.

With actionable advice, real-world examples, and practical tools, this book will help readers learn the skills and strategies necessary to unleash their business online and maximize their online presence.

What's in it for you?

Unleash Your Business Online is an invaluable resource for businesses of all sizes looking to grow their online presence. It contains best practices, practical advice, and real-world examples from successful businesses on how to effectively utilize the latest digital marketing tools, strategies, and technologies. The book provides a comprehensive overview of the latest trends and developments, and will help you understand the importance of having a strong online presence in order to stay competitive in today's digital world. It also covers topics such as search engine optimization, content marketing, social media marketing, email marketing, and more. With step-by-step instructions, this book will help you unleash your business online and take it to the next level.

Unleash Your Business Online will help you identify the right channels, the right approach, the right tools, and we don't stop there. I will make sure that by the end of this book, you will have a store online. This is a two-way process, of course, but I assure you that from my side, I have invested my blood, sweat, tears into getting you prepared.

Make the most of this book and join my online course," Grand Launch Academy," where you will get to network with like-minded individuals who are also all set to take their business to another level. In our group, you will regularly update the new trends, tools, and strategies that emerge every day in the digital world. You wouldn't want to miss out on that!

See you inside!

Empowering Quote #1

Brand Building is the Ultimate way of Wealth creation- Shubham Bapna.

Chapter One

Changing the Mindset

Eeveryone around us has a biased understanding of how things should work and how things will work. That's not wrong. This unique understanding of things that we call the "mindset" is cultivated through various incidences, events, and circumstances that might have occurred to them during their lifetime. Before we dive hard into this book, you need to promise me something. Today, you're going to be open to change.

Why do we need to change the mindset? Unleashing your business online is dependent on a new idea, new strategies. When we function with the old ones, there is a high possibility that our thoughts will clash, which will make things difficult further down the road. I suggest you must follow and understand this chapter thoroughly.

This chapter will help you unlearn, learn, find the outcomes, plan a roadmap, measure your progress, and implement the learnings. Are you ready for that? Let's get started.

Changing your Mindset

I always wanted to travel the world, explore unknown places. From the "heart coming out of my chest" feeling you get while indulging in the many adventurous activities in Queenstown, to the "melting me heart softly" feeling you get while driving around the European country roads, I wanted to explore them all!

Does this sound unachievable? Perhaps, scary?

Before your subconscious mind jumps right in and starts reasoning how and why you can't do this, let me tell you something. The possibilities are endless. You can achieve all the things you've ever dreamt of, all the things that motivate you to get out of bed every morning, all the possibilities. You need to change your beliefs and start transforming your thought process. Start wondering, imagining, manifesting, and creating all you've wanted in your mind. When you start thinking that this is undoubtedly not something that is out of your control, I'll be honest; it will cost you money. But you will be able to afford it.

Let's break the pattern now. Whenever a "you can't do this" marches in on your mind, replace it with a beautiful image of your future. So before anything, let's cut short that negative thought process right about now.

A new thought process will transform you enough to understand all the concepts I'll be narrating for unleashing your business online. Changing your mindset is not that tough. Let me tell you what you need to do to bring a thorough change to your mindset.

Unlearn.

Unlearning is an essential concept that, somehow, people associate as something negative. A need that should be practiced almost every day gets passed on with a shrug and a "tch." What happens when I talk about unlearning? And how is this related to unleashing your business online? You might be a successful business person with millions of dollars in turnover in revenue through your offline channel, but now with the inception of

COVID, how are you keeping up?

So now, the question arises – Can we take up our business online during this crisis?

Going Online is Mandatory for every Business Owner. We are seeing those numbers rising in comparison to the earlier years. You should always have multiple channels to grow your business exponentially and expand to places. Companies in the West are using this every single day. So, why are we missing out? Why are we waiting for an external incident to occur to understand the importance of growing our business and having different streams of reaching our customers?

This entire book is about turning your offline business into an online empire. After reading this book, you will get a massive breakthrough. It will give you a fantastic transformation, which will lead you to a successful future in your business and personal life.

First things first, let's understand how to unlearn. Start compartmentalizing. All the other thoughts and teaching that you've learned till now keep them aside. You have one thing to do, and that is not to mix up these concepts. Our goal is to channelize all the learnings and use it together to our advantage. You need to have a clear mindset. When you move ahead with a clear mindset, you will be shocked to see how fast you can grasp the new terminologies and ideas that I'll share in this book.

Learn.

Regular learning helps to bring out the best ideas back to the business. Keep your mind open; keep them coming. Build a mindset that allows you to accept all the facts. Keep your hands free, your heart open, and your mind open. It's super important. Okay, now let's put a full stop to the philosophy.

The concepts that I'll be teaching you are widely available in the World Wide Web, but they are not structured. If I had to name one life-changing hack that I learned over the years, it would be the lesson of "thinking in a structured way." I have learned this the hard way. I had browsed through multiple trainings, multiple books, numerous blogs, and articles all over the internet when I had just started. I've seen a crazy amount of videos to understand what was happening, why it was happening, and how the outcome would be. When I was studying different digital marketing concepts to grow my family business and my new ventures online, the most crucial question was, why and how.

How would I do that? I have zero knowledge about it.

How will I get deep into it, understand the concepts, and make myself a successful business person?

What did I do? My head was occupied with such thoughts

all day long. First, I started defining the outcomes, planting a roadmap. Rather than looking at your goals from a distance, zoom in a little bit, and start creating small destinations— Point A, Point B, and so on. Where I would reach the place I want to achieve was from point A to point B. That's how I got started. And as I've learned in multiple business meetings, that specific is terrific.

Find the Outcomes

Once I understand that I have to be very specific, I have to be very specific about where I am goinThis will help me know that reaching from point A to point B is accessible, achievable, and it will help me get started. So what did I do? I started noting down, planning out in a very systematic way, experimenting with each of the concepts during my trial and error method. With that, I was able to achieve a proper path that anyone, I repeat, anyone in this world who have their business offline can make. Even with little presence online, this book can unleash your business potential on the digital platform. Are you ready? I'm pretty sure you are. Since you have reached this level, you must understand the "unlearn- learn" method, defining the outcomes, and planning a roadmap. How do you plan to achieve that with a systematic process? With the intricately crafted assignments, I'll be giving you.

Planning a Roadmap

In this book, you will be able to measure your progress and implement all the learnings efficiently. Right from the moment you complete the chapters, respectively, you will get an idea of how these things can help you get started with a new business, finding new job opportunities, and also help you in mentoring other entrepreneurs. If you can mentor other entrepreneurs out there into unleashing their business online, that's a sign that you're headed towards the right path. And that's my sign to realize that I am successful, too. What can be a better outcome than to help other entrepreneurs in growing and providing all their facilities to the world?

Decide a proper roadmap by following a systematic plan. With the help of this, you will be able to achive all that is mentioned in this. For real. Measure your Progress

The best way to measure their progress in the business world is through one straightforward method, i.e., the direct approach. When you're implementing something, it helps you to get an idea of how things work in real life. You can understand how it will work out in a real business sense. Getting started is very important. This book is not just for you to read and keep aside. You will reap the most out of this book only when you're able to implement and take action. The action-oriented approach will help you make the most out of this book. If you're facing any difficulties in implementing these things, you can always discuss it in our Mastermind group. Just check out www.grandlaunch.co, you'll find the link to Grand Launch Academy, join that group. As I say, you need to define the outcomes of where you want to reach.

Implement the Learnings

Being specific is going to take you towards terrific results, the results you have always wanted to have, but something inside you kept stopping you from achieving it until now. This book can be the book that breaks all the barriers that prevent you from reaching your future. This book is much more than just unleashing your business online. I know how it feels to be you, to think that no matter what you do, you are stagnant in one place as if some glue has been purposefully stuck on the back of your shoe. Don't worry, I, herby, assure you that no power can ever stop you from building your empire, from taking the first step towards unleashing your business online.

If you've noticed, I've been repeating the sentence "Unleash your business online" for quite some time now, and I'll be doing that in all the chapters coming ahead too. The idea behind it is to plant in your mind the seed that you can unleash your business online and break the mindset. Change the mindset that has clung into your brain, the mindset that blocks you from achieving all the positive things that you rightfully deserve, the many potential opportunities outside your spectrum that are just waiting for you to come and get a hold of them.

So what did we learn from this chapter? We learned the importance of changing our mindset, unlearn and then learning, defining the outcomes, planning a roadmap, measuring progress, and implementing these learnings to take you to the destination you want to reach.

Empowering Quote #2

Content Curation is more potent than Content Creation- Shubham Bapna.

Chapter Two

Understanding the possibilities.

What are the possibilities of your venture turning into a success after implementing the digital strategies mentioned here?

More importantly, when do you start seeing those possibilities?

You need to analyze your business, understand your business, and keep track of your competitors daily. We will know how you can track your competitors who are seemingly doing a great business online and take the right steps to compete with them and define the possibilities for your business and yourself.

Simple things right?

When I talk about possibilities, I can't leave without taking an example of a brand that we have all used and confided in at some point in our life. I'm talking about none other than Amazon. Amazon is an internet-based company that saw its inception in mid-1994. Amazon coming into the picture, made the whole world perceive e-commerce differently. It was going to take business away from all those incumbent businesses that were too reluctant to provide more exceptional customer service to the very customers that were the backbone of their company.

When looking at those Incumbent companies, Adapting to future technologies was not something in their forte. Mr. Jeff Bezos was very much aware of this, and hence we took advantage of it. He understood that there was a possibility of Amazon becoming a glorious success because it catered to what people wanted, and what they wanted was a higher possibility of purchasing things online. This was without having to find them out by visiting the stores or without having to wait for the stock to come in.

The comfort level that Amazon provided in those days was something no other company could match. There was a possibility that Amazon can take over the world in the retail e-commerce section. Retail e-commerce was booming then, it was booming right there. And over the next coming years, it started taking over the world.

How was this the case?

How was Amazon able to go and become an e-commerce giant?

Now, it has even touched a *trillion-dollar*market cap. How did Jeff Bezos and Amazon look into these possibilities? Let's understand how it works.

First of all, what you need to understand is that your business is scalable, and a lot is achievable. But for that, you need to map out five simple things. Let's get started.

- What is your business all about?

- Who are your competitors?

- Who is your target audience?

- Is your target audience online?

- Is your target audience buying things online?

Having an understanding of this is critical because if you plan on *Unleashing your business online*, then your customer must first be online. Only, then all these things will be helpful for you. Let's assume that you are into building supplies. You're supplying cement; you're providing all the elements needed to construct a house, a building, or a factory. You place your business up online only to find out that your customers are not on it.

What do you do? How do you plan to approach them?

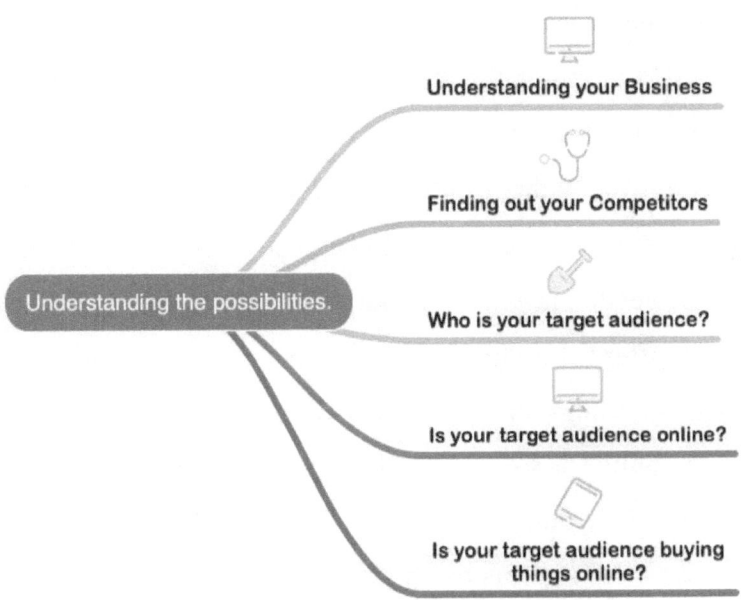

Understanding your Business

Finding out your Competitors

Understanding the possibilities.

Who is your target audience?

Is your target audience online?

Is your target audience buying things online?

Simple steps to find out how Online growth strategies can suit your Business

A simple way of approaching them can be via people who are handling transactions online and are in business related to your target audience. They can be real estate brokers; they can be architects. They can be anyone who falls into this business relationship. You can target these people and make them connect with your target audience instead. Using this will help you achieve a more significant business by providing incentives to those who are online.

Now that you know what to do, let's focus on how to do it, shall we?

How can you structure this?

A quick recap, you're a building supplier, you also sell cement. Looking at this context, you can assume your target audience are builders. There are two ways of targeting them: either you focus them directly or choose the "via" method to target them through people in the industry. You can ask them to help you get connected with your real target audience. This way, you can offer the architects or the agents, some incentives, or a referral commission. And this way, you can expand your business online as well. With this, you will gain a multi- channel approach, i.e., online as well as offline. This way, you can achieve all the success that you have ever wanted by applying this principle along with the other laws that will follow in the coming chapters.

Simply follow those five simple steps as listed above, plan out and chalk down the plan. Make your business idea very simple, very structured, and in no time will you understand the possibilities that are lying ahead of you. All you need to do is to grab them and seize the opportunities. Take on the challenges to achieve all that you ever wanted, right at this very moment.

My company, _Grand Launch_, helps a lot of business individuals to increase their sales using all these strategies exponentially. My forum guides business owners to take on all the challenges and turn them into opportunities, just by using all the mentioned steps in this book. You can apply this to your business as well.

You can take on these challenges and turn them into money-generating machines. You can expand to multiple business networks and various countries, mark your presence there, make your business thrive exponentially, and grow continuously.

Every multinational company has implemented this, so why not you?

You can also achieve them. All you need to do is have a structured approach and have a mindset that allows the people around you to follow a similar pattern.

Many business owners ask me if I have any network or people around me.

The answer is Yes. Once you find like-minded people around you, you automatically and unknowingly start honing your skills. If you're friends with other business owners, you can observe the issues they're facing and, by that, avoid the same mistakes they have been doing all their life. You can help each other grow offline as well as online. I run a Mastermind network, where we help business owners like you, expand their business online using my carefully curated digital strategies through the digital medium. This Mastermind involves a lot of brainstorming and a lot of understanding of what strategy can be useful for a particular business. Every month we meet, depending on the conditions and we are present all over the world. You can join this network and find out the possibilities and opportunities lying ahead for you. For more information, you can check out my website,

www.unleashyourbusiness.online, or check out my website called www.shubhambapna.com.

Empowering Quote #3

Without Systematic Digital Marketing, no
Business can Survive- Shubham Bapna.

Chapter Three

Analyzing your business.

Once you understand your business prospects, you know how your business works, and how your business can scale online. It will become effortless for you to adapt and take on all the new learnings from this book and implement it in a short time. A lot of people who succeed by understanding the system that I'm trying to explain right here are the ones who have analyzed and understood their business very well.

So, how do you analyze your business?

The number one way is to draw a map and clear out the USPs of your company when you're trying to get it online. There are a lot of competitors online that are doing exceptionally well for themselves. In such a scenario, your USP is what's going to make you stand out. You need to find out what makes your business unique, and what's the selling point for your business.

There are a lot of tools that can help you build a better business model. Let me list them down for you.

One can be Plan cruncher, visual mapping, integration cards, proposition blueprint, Business Model Canvas, or even the Lean canvas. You can find all of these in the link called *www.unleashyourbusiness.online.* You can find all the support over there; you can download them and get an idea of how you can plan out much better so that you can succeed without having any issues with the trial and error method.

I had followed a similar pattern in starting my new Automated Affiliate Platform called Suprcrowd. Suprcrowd is a digital platform that helps business owners and freelancers list their business online. While I was validating the idea and understanding how this will work, it was essential for me to get through the lean canvas model and understand the business idea in a much better sense. After a proper analysis, it helps me plan out how to raise funds from external investors.

And you know what? Foreign investors prefer this much more over the large pages in the PPT. Let me put it out there, we all secretly know PPTs can sometimes really confuse us rather than solving our problems. That's how we need to analyze your business model when you're planning to go online. You need to find - the problem, the solution, the key metrics, the unique value proposition, the unfair advantage that cannot be copied or bought quickly, and the channels, i.e., the path through which your customer will buy online. It can be via your website or an eCommerce platform. It can be through Suprcrowd too.

Next,

- Who is your customer target segment? *You need to identify that.*

- What is going to be the cost structure?

- What is your revenue stream going to look like?

- What is your revenue model?

- What is its lifetime value?

- How much money are you spending on hosting?

- For bringing the customers CAC (Customer Acquisition Cost)?

Answering all these questions will help you get a clear idea of how you can plan out without disturbing your offline business. Your online market is going to be an extension of your actual business. But this extension cannot be similar to your offline business. You need to analyze the right steps, the right strategies, and if you ever need any help apart from this book, you can always contact our team. You can still get in touch with me. You will understand the power of our Mastermind group, where people around the world can help you get started and chip in all the needs, all the help that you ever wanted.

The power of a Mastermind can help you in all such activities. Such a group can help you identify the help you need, and vice versa. Most importantly, when you've grabbed control of the various strategies that your competitors are using, you can do business better than them. Using such a method can also make your company rank high among your customers.

When you plan to start your business, first, what you need to do is identify what your competitors are doing. And for that, you need to identify who your competitors are. Not just the popular ones, you must look at all your competitors equally. Some may not have established themselves well now, but you never know when they'll come to snatch the 1ˢᵗ prize.

Asking the right questions will help you get the best answers. To understand this better, of course, we must start with an example. Let's assume you are Shopify, a platform that enables business owners to create their storefronts. Enabling

Business Owners to create their Storefronts is mainly a similar service that you might be providing.

This way, your customers sell their products and services through your platform by having that integrated with their domain name. Now when we look into this business, doesn't it sound like a Software-as-a-Service (SaaS) business? There would be competitors in this field, as well. Ecommerce SaaS is a very lucrative industry, as more and more companies are considering setting up their store online and moving fiercely towards such platforms. Now comes the entry of your competitor; let's assume its name is "Big Commerce." Big Commerce is eating up the market, and I'm sure that the way they have studied their competitor, i.e., you, is helping them gain market share and improve their business skills.

What to do in such a case?

We use the same pattern and similar scale strategies that all the businesses around the world are using. That way, you can identify your competitors, determine what kind of approach they're using, and what type of planning they would be coming up with to do the business. With this much of insight, you can improve your top line, your bottom line, the way you function, and the best part, you can OWN the market. Remember that when you create your business online, everything becomes pretty transparent.

Now that you know the importance of Competitor analysis, let me run you through the different metrics that we will be using to get going. Competitor analysis is identifying what your customer wants, and which competitor is giving that.

The first thing we tend to do is conduct a SWOT analysis. We identify the different frameworks that affects our business, i.e., the internal and external factors (as your strength and weaknesses) and then identify the threats and opportunities lying ahead. While at it, you get to understand yourself as well as your competition. When we are doing competitive analysis in detail, we look into the product or service they're selling, the kind of cost structure that they're following, the financial services, marketing strategies, strengths, weaknesses, business model, subscription, and so on so forth.

You do this analysis by identifying at least five to six competitors in your space, which will enable you to find out what you would like to replicate. This way, you can spend an ample amount of time planning and making sure to give your 200% so that when you put in your time, money, and energy, there is a high possibility of your product or service gaining a high market share with a consistent cash flow.

A simple way to start your competitor analysis is by making a Google Sheet and a Google document file. Both Google Sheet & Excel are available online, with which you can track and do your work, share it with your teammates, and work on a real-time basis.

First, identify your competitors.

They can be in direct or indirect competition to your business. Next, determine the criteria on which you're taking your goal and scope in the picture. With this, you will be able to find out their features, weaknesses, value proposition, the type of content and tone they're using, and even things like the business managers they're following on social media. The last thing you must do is to interrogate your clients. Ask them who they would go for if you shut down your business. This way, you can identify your best possible competitor.

Isn't it a fantastic way to identify how you can look into your competitors, analyze your business, and make sure that the kind of strategies that you would be following would help you in getting your business started? Not only that, but this can also help in scaling and unleashing your business online, which is the focus of this book. This book has a real understanding of how you can do this in a very systematic and grand manner.

Let's assume you have carefully done your competitor analysis. Now you have to figure out how you can be better than your competition. This process is more straightforward than you think. Always remember that customers look for value for money. That means that if your competitor is providing X+1, you must provide X+1+2. Offer more value for the same or less money, and see your competitors go crazy. This way, you can capture the market, grow your market share, increase your revenue, and have a high ROI compared to the expenses you would incur. This first step will help you more than you think in the future. For starters, it will help with increasing your online presence and help you understand how to analyze your business systematically.

In the next chapter, we will understand precisely that. How can you achieve an online presence? I'll provide a chart and a checklist too. We will be covering a lot of things ahead. Make sure you read and note down all that you find is important.

Empowering Quote #4

Brand Building is the Ultimate way of Creating
Wealth Online- Shubham Bapna

Chapter Four

Getting your Online presence ready.

First and foremost, when I say online presence, I mean that you need to have a website, a social media presence, capture the places where your customers frequent, and the kind of industry your business is working in.

- Domain Name
- Email
- Website Design
- Hosting
- Logo
- Social Media
- Content

Getting your Online presence ready.

Basic checklist to get your Onilne Presence ready

Domain Name

Domain's name is ".com" ".in," basically what you see at the end of every website. It is also known as "TLD," i.e., Top Level Domain. There are more than 1500 TLDs to choose from. With so many options, which one should you choose? There are many factors that you need to look into when deciding the TLD you would go for. It can be .museum, .biz, .info, .network, .museum, .pro, .vip and so on. But the most common and the most likely to be identified by Google search engines and your customers are - .com .co, .co.in, .co.us. The Domain name TLD also depends on the kind of business that you are into. If you're creating a website for a museum, ".museum" will be the most suitable.

The more comfortable your domain name, the easier it is for your brand to grow regularly.

Email

Let's assume you are Suprcrowd, which is my Automated Affiliate Platform btw. Mostly, you will have to make two email ids. First is the primary id from which most of your emails will go. It can also be set as hello@suprcrowd.in. Every established company has its customer care. For a support based email, i.e., for customer care, your id must be something like - support@suprcrowd.in. Having such an email makes it easy for your customers to track you, and if at all, if they want to talk to you, they'll know where to contact. A branded email gives you a lot of credibility. If your customers receive emails from unsolicited parties at all, they'll be able to differentiate and identify you.

Website Design

Your website is your storefront; it's your online presence. It's everything that you will have online. Therefore, you must invest in it carefully and make sure that all your money that is going into it is making it attractive. When you're going for a website, there are plenty of things you must consider. The kind of color scheme you will be going for, the type of fonts that you will be using, they have to be by your business.

If you have a corporate customer base, colors like blue, white, gray, will make your website look professional. If you're into art, music, dance, then funky colors are the way to go. They bring out creativity. If you are into online coaching, color schemes with the range of black or white, even light blue or light pink color will suit them best. Colour schemes are relevant; they are the first thing your customers notice and unconsciously judge you on. It shows that your business reflects the kind of website you are displaying to them. The colors, the fonts, the placements, the captions, the H1 tag, the copy, and the captions play an essential role in capturing your visitor's attention.

Hosting

To get started with a website, you must choose a host. A host is a platform that allows individuals to make their website accessible on the World Wide Web. The most widely used platform is Wix. GoDaddy, Bluehost, Hostgator, etc. are also close competitors.

If you're planning for a simple website, I suggest you go for WordPress. But if you're planning to get a lot of visitors, then having a WordPress website can also have a lot of adverse effects. Your site can crash since WordPress only allows enough bandwidth that, unfortunately, cannot take a heavy load. Chances of your website getting corrupted due to a few plugins, is also high. A lot of times, you need to update those plugins to keep your website functioning. And this can be difficult, especially if you're not that active in managing your website thoroughly.

Making a website is pretty simple but can also be time-consuming. There are many YouTube tutorials for it, but you can also choose to get it done from the digital agencies. We have handled 100 plus websites for business coaches, companies, brands, celebrities, and have also helped them gain traffic, by optimizing their website and making it ready for SEO. Coming to SEO, we will be studying this in detail in future chapters. For now, let's cover the last few points on getting your online presence ready.

Logo

Now that we have built a website, it's time to get a logo. A logo is a small design that helps in identifying your brand. Your logo should speak about your business, and a tagline is also highly recommended. A slogan reflects your business idea in one line and does not have more than six to eight words.

"An Automated Affiliate Platform" is the tagline for my company, Suprcrowd. It's short, simple, and speaks about my business. Deciding on a worthy slogan will help chalk out the kind of understanding that I need to create for my visitors and anyone looking into my brand, logo, or social media graphics, and help them identify what this platform, what this name stands for.

Since I'm creating a brand, there's so much more which has to be done. The color scheme you use is of high significance here. If I'm going for something very formal, I need to have white, black, gray, light blue, etc. in my palette. If I want my brand to ooze out an energetic presence, I'll use orange, yellow, and shades of red. The colors must be subtle but enough to grab attention. What is common between Twitter, LinkedIn, and Facebook? Yes, you guessed that right. All of them use light blue and its shades in their logo. But why? Every color speaks. In light blue, it gives out the impression of reliability, making them automatically look trustable.

On the other hand, if you see the color used for Instagram, we must say it's quite dynamic. It's colorful, playful, and very different from its affiliate, Facebook. Instagram wants to show that it's vivid and full of energy, and we must say it's a mission success. Colors play an essential role in branding and building your presence online.

Social Media

Online presence is almost synonymous to having social media accounts nowadays. You need to have your social media presence on Facebook, Instagram, LinkedIn, Twitter, Quora, Tik-Tok, YouTube, Pinterest, and others. So many platforms to indulge in. You don't necessarily have to use all the platforms. It also depends on the kind of business you're doing. Think of it like this – If your customer is a man in his late 20s who likes to frequent at Restobars, will you go looking for him at McDonald's? The same goes for online.

Let's say you are into a B2B business. If so, your social media preferred platform could be LinkedIn, Quora, YouTube, and even Twitter. There is a high possibility that you can capture your target audience there and redirect them to your website. Let's put a check on social media accounts. Now, it's time to get some graphics ready. Graphics are creative images that you set as your cover or in your posts over social media to convey your message. Since this is not a one-off thing that you can just isolate once the work is done, most companies contact digital agencies. If you have the time to create graphics daily, you can use websites like Canva or Crello, too, free and have readymade templates.

Content

Your website is ready; your Social Media accounts have been fired up; the graphics are prepared to be uploaded.

Now what?

You need a systematic presentation to bind all these together, right?

That's content. A simple trick, you don't have to break your head around making content for each channel. Once you've built the content, it can remain standard across all the social media platforms.

Taking the example of my Automated Affiliate Platform, again, the content we put on social media platforms was straightforward. The tagline is your Automated Affiliate Platform that comes with advanced eCommerce tools that you can start for free. So this line was we were gaining a lot of traffic when starting our own. We launched this platform recently, on the first week of June. And since then, a lot of customers have joined our platform. So these are the benefits of having a proposed plan and strategy in place when you're going for your online business and online presence ready to get started.

You need to understand how you can build your email list, how you can master the SEO part, how you can have a proper content planning done. How you can personify your brand, and how you can contact influencers to help you market your brand. How you can develop relationships with different brands, who are in line with your business, can act as a relationship referrals.

Relationship referrals are something that helps us to connect with Business Owners having similar customers. They are certainly not into the same industry. Since we are into digital marketing and information technology, relationship referrals could be Common business owners, compliance managers, or even a lot of business SMEs, large businesses. Any connections from them can help my business to grow online as well as offline.

It is essential to build relationships online. But is there a social media platform that can help you with that?

Of course. LinkedIn can be beneficial for your business. But with this platform, please remember that you need to identify your relationship referrals that can help you generate much better traffic than any other platform. You can also try to join a few business groups, which can help you connect with like-minded people faster. You can search for such groups on Reddit, LinkedIn, Facebook, etc. Here's hoping you've got a clear idea of what you can do and why it is essential. See you in the next chapter.

Empowering Quote #5

Without a proper marketing strategy, even a great product can fail- Shubham Bapna.

Chapter Five

Creating your business story.

Everything becomes more interesting once you get to know the story behind it. Once you've successfully created an online presence, the next step is to create an account. A business story is all about the what, why, and how of your business.

- Why do you want to grow your business online?

- What are your business objectives?

- What is the story behind your business?

- How are you different from your competitors?

- What is your value offering compared to your Competitors?

Contrary to popular opinion, a customer-business relationship is not just about buying and selling. If that was the case, why do customers have their favorites among so many options? The questions asked above are what is going to make you stand out amongst the crowd. Your website must be able to answer all these questions very well. You need to dedicate a whole page for just that. An "About Us" page on your website will do just that for you. This page is where every business can tell their story, timeline, team players, who their leaders are, what their USP is, their mission, and their vision behind the company. This helps your visitors identify your key metrics, the critical areas of the business as well as get to know the things that your visitors care about.

So what are the things that visitors care about? The visitors coming to your website will always care about what they will get in return for the commercial value that they're you. You can be into the business of selling products, services; you can be a consultant too. Your website must explain your products/services well.

When you visit my website, you can see a clear call to action. Call to work is a term that we, digital marketers commonly use to induce a viewer to perform buying or revisit our website. It can be "call now," "book now," "sale," or any such thing that attracts the attention of the visitor. This can help you in improving your funnel and getting clarity for your website.

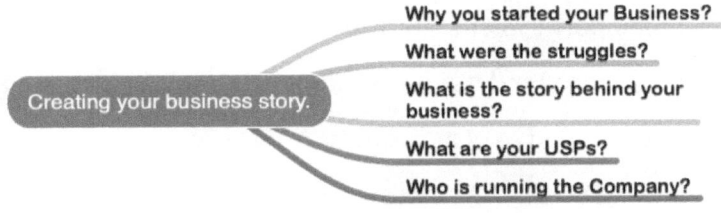

A strong Business story can make a Business much more successful.

Building your story helps you gain more customers, increase your revenue, increase the traffic that you might receive on your website, and portray your customers who you are, what you do, and why you want to do it. All of this needs to be planned and written down in a structured manner, or your website will just end up looking like a mess. So to do that, you need to have a clear idea about your business first. Your business story needs to be relatable, and your website should be able to show just that.

Let's say you're into the business of fresh juices. You're selling new and packaged juice online.

Do you know what your visitors are going to search for first? Your expertise?

Your experience?

The team that is handling the business? What are their Credentials?

What type of distribution channels are you having?

The support system from the government, your food and beverage license, and any other thing that will help you build credibility around your business? You can also rope in influencers, actors, and ambassadors who can help you market your product, who can be the face of your brand and help you gain much more audience.

This audience will help you connect with the youth, with the public out there, so that your brand can get a lot of awareness and marketing that it needs to help grow. You can also contact the public release or PR agencies to help you spread the news about your brand. PR will create a lot of positive impact. Such kind of features and benefits can help your potential customers could receive when they consume or take your products and services into consideration.

Story building is a continuous process, and your ROI will help you find out which direction it is leading you to. You can also identify the critical point that enables you to be different from your competitors, which you can eventually use to define your position in the market. That's an effortless way to build your story online. Another way to build your story online is to collect testimonials.

Testimonials in the form of videos of your loyal customers can get up your game. Imagine opening a website and being greeted with videos of real customers giving real testimonials. In just a matter of a minute, the brand will seem more familiar to you even though you don't want to give in. Even if you leave the website and forget it for a few days, the next time you're in need, this is the brand that you'll immediately recall and would want to put your trust in. It gives your potential customers an idea that this is what their outcome will be when they receive a product from your company. Such can be how you can build your online credibility and an online story on your platform. When I say platform, I also mean the different social media platforms you'll use and not just your website. You can also have backlinking, which is a part of SEO, but we will be covering that later on.

Empowering Quote #6

Businesses can survive and thrive if the new growth strategies are adopted- Shubham

Bapna.

Chapter Six

Identifying the right strategies.

Before we get started, I would like to break one myth. There is no such thing as a perfect strategy for an online business. Every business requires different approaches and alignments of those strategies to build a high sales funnel. You will find the right plan eventually after going through numerous trial and error methods.

To identify the right strategy for you, I have compiled 30 different tips and 30 different ways. Leverage the data and make the most out of this.

Right steps to Unleash your Business Online

Don't copy

You must not blatantly copy other entrepreneurs. Their strategies are limited to their business. What works for them will not work you. It will be worse if you go full-fledged into their plan, only to realize that it didn't work for them either.

Never, I repeat, never go around copying other businesses. No amount of revenue or ROI is going to define if a strategy is right.

Keep it Simple

Digitization has given birth to so many different tools, tactics, and strategies. It's natural to be lost in between them, which is why keeping things simple becomes even more critical as the day passes. There are chances that you may several inputs and suggestions since it's your first time going online. But I request you not to pay heed to them because it's you who will incur costs in the end for the many mistakes, not them. Keep your strategies simple and to the point. Go ahead and make a business plan according to the lean canvas model. I love it.

Just make sure that your website is simple to scroll through and that there is a proper call to action everywhere you post. You'll know your strategy works when you see the apparent interest in getting created among your customers. My point is that if that's successfully happening, create a similar plan with only a few modifications. These modifications can be elementary. Change the way you write your ads, maybe add different words the next time, add different colors, add bonuses and discounts, change the pricing. And if this strategy works better for you, make this the primary one. As I mentioned earlier, trial and error are going to lead the way for you to find your perfect strategy.

Be Honest

Social media is a two-blade sword. Either it can help and make you the winner, or it can kill you. Your reputation is fragile and could be damaged within a few hours if something negative goes viral. You won't believe some pages are dedicatedly running online to analyze who copied who online and calling them out. Keep in mind to avoid plagiarism.

Make your ad copies pure, honest, precise. Help your customers figure out how much they need your brand. This will not only help you gain credibility in your customer's eyes but will also generate a lot of traction over some time. It's a whole lot better to maintain your online reputation in the inertia phase itself rather than resorting to an online reputation management later on, isn't it?

Generate Credibility

As discussed in the previous chapter, having testimonials is essential. Your online credibility will come through testimonials. They can be in the form of videos, quotes, commands, pictures, etc. Place the testimonials on your front page. Let your customers advertise you for a change.

Testimonials are the best when they come in a video format. So ask your customers to help you, and I'm pretty sure they would love to be a part of your branding too. They'll be thrilled to be on the front page of your website and might even ask their friends and family to visit your site just to see them.

Offer Limited Options

In a world where every business is giving its most to the customers by offering a hundred thousand options to choose from for starters, it is natural to feel the need to do the same. I am no genie to predict what goes wrong, but I will put my bets on this tight – Have you ever experienced the frustration of a customer leading you on? Showing so much interest in the beginning and then leaving you hanging like that. You will know that they are initially very much interested in they are very fascinated to see so many options. Still, at the same time, they're now more confused than ever, and the worst part, they might even plan on exploring a competitor's brand, now that you've let their interest escalate to a whole different level. The more the options, the higher the confusion in your customer's mind, and this will break down your sales drastically.

Don't give them too many options. Stick to a number and limit yourself there, but make sure you're giving them the best. And how do you know what's best? By doing a competitor analysis. See what your competition is providing and use the X+1+2 method. Lastly, structure the products on your website in a very systematic manner. Easy to track, simpler to scroll.

Refund Policy

Refund policy builds trust in the mind of your customer. By giving a significant refund, your customer will rest assured and not mind paying you, not once but multiple times. Trust builds loyalty. In no time, they will come back to your ecosystem again.

A Simple Checkout Process

Nowadays, there have been many complaints about how customers face the most problems, especially when they're checking out. To the point that they even find queueing up in a line at a physical store better. Did you know that there is a 21% chance that your customer will abandon you if the checkout process is complicated? Last year alone, $4 trillion of Online sales was lost due to cart abandonment, alone. Here the figure could have been quickly recovered if they had fixed the bug at the right time.

Payment Options

Payment options differ from country to country. But if I talk about India, the kind of payment options that we prefer are UPI, credit cards, debit cards, and wallets. Net Banking is still not prevalent here. But if I am in the B2B industry, net banking as an option would be highly perceived and acceptable. Such payment solutions usually depends on the kind of audience you're catering to. In general, going for Razor pay, Stripe, PayPal, Paytm, and other such payment gateway providers is preferable. Your payment option will look streamlined and will be safe and secure. Nothing can create a lot of distrust in your customers than having a lousy payment gateway.

Nowadays, a lot of these payment gateways provide the option of automated receipts. Optimization can be attained with the help of digital tools available or different applications, e.g., Pabbly Connect, Pabbly, Quickwork, etc. I'll explain more on this app later.

Activate your Social Media Account

Your social media account allows you to disseminate all the information you want to give. Social media is the only platform where people will willingly see your posts. You can post pictures, videos on your business, your story, the kind of progress that your business is doing, and a lot of different things that define your business. In the era of all things digital, you will lag if you aren't active on social media. An active social media account attracts followers, who may not be a fan of your products but are there for the content. A large amount of audiences can be targeted on a digital platform. This will help in business growth and directly redirect your customers to the website, thereby helping to generate traffic.

Email Marketing

Emails are an asset to any online business. You cannot ignore email marketing because that's the best and the most efficient way of getting connected and staying connected with your customers. You must realize that there are many distractions online. To keep in the back of your customers' minds, you must always maintain regular contact with them. Emails are the best way to execute that. You can send a sequence of emails over days and months, which can generate curiosity over some time. It has the highest ROI since the cost of sending emails is very, very low.

Emails come with unlimited plans, the only limitation being that there is a cap on the number of subscribers. I would suggest you to go for SendFox, ConvertKit and more such email marketing software. These email marketing plans will help keep your budget tight and let you send unlimited emails that inform your customers about new offers, new products, strategies, services, etc. An excellent way to keep your audience interested is by sharing your behind-the-scene stories on email.

Create Videos

Using videos as a medium to generate traffic can increase your reach and help you gain conversions on your website. Videos can be about your business, your products, and features. It can also be topical; you can create short videos on festivals or something that your business can complement to. In case you're into the sports industry, you can post pictures and videos on the upcoming sportsperson, you can collaborate with influencers in the same field. By the way, we will touch upon influencer marketing in detail later.

Create share-worthy videos. It does not have to highlight your business only. Short videos attract more attention than pictures nowadays.

Create a Lead Magnet

A lead magnet is a strategy where you can provide something for free in exchange for customer information. This way, you can collect their emails, their name, their mobile number, and add them to your autoresponder. What is an autoresponder? Autoresponder is the same term we use for an email marketing software.

The best part about this is that you're getting the information voluntarily. And as mentioned in the email marketing point, you can engage these potential customers by sharing your new launch, products, or even by sharing your stories. This will help you generate traffic on your platform.

Graphics

As I have mentioned earlier, having graphics that reflect your business, will help your business connect with your audience deeply. But me repeating this once again should hopefully show you the importance of it.

Using your photos and videos will allow you to have a sense of customization. It will look professional as well as help in avoiding copyrights and other legal issues. Having personal photos of individuals are required to be given credit. If you're having pictures taken of your products or your services that are being used by your customers, then you can get them by way of testimonials and use them on your platform. This will help you generate a sense of authenticity, as well as create a trust in the minds of the customers.

Join a Network Group

If you face any difficulty, you can always join my Mastermind group. We discuss all the strategies listed above in- depth, identify which ones are working for whom, and implement those in our businesses. If you feel like you're the right candidate, and want to be surrounded with like-minded people who meet or interact regularly online, offline, discuss strategies, and grasp knowledge, increasing their business on a massive scale, you should join my Mastermind group. You can contact this link called www.unleashyourbusiness. online/Mastermind. You will get a lot of information over there. This way, you can join the best possible Mastermind group on this planet, which can help your business gain an exponential online growth that you've always desired.

Empowering Quote #7

To grow any Business exponentially, one must use Business automation tools- Shubham Bapna.

Chapter Seven

Little Known Growth Hacks.

What can be the little known growth hack that can help you generate more business, increase your following, and have a consistent flow of business for your venture? Number One way is to have a link to a more extensive website.

Let me take an example of PayPal and eBay. PayPal was overgrowing its competitors yet; it was struggling a lot in terms of losing money to x.com. This was the company being run by Mr. Elon Musk. What did PayPal do? PayPal partnered with eBay by becoming their preferred payment platform. That allowed eBay to increase its transactions and conversions, while PayPal was getting the most benefit. PayPal benefited the most by increasing its user base exponentially. Such an expansion led to a reduction in the cost as well as an increase in the cart value. This way, PayPal had gained a lot of customers over the years and an audience that helped them become a multi-billion dollar brand.

How can you use this in your business strategies? You can

use this little known growth hack by partnering with a biggie in the industry or partnering with complement business persons. By partnering with them, you will have their audience and their customer base, but you will also get access to a broader audience, which can be of great potential by increasing the user base for both the business owners.

The second one can be wild marketing. Who wouldn't want to go viral in these times? Going viral can lead to a more considerable increase in revenue as well as brand value. Let's take the example of Dollar Shave Club, where they introduced their new $1 blades that have now gained a massive audience. They used viral marketing by making a funny video. It showed all their features and helped them achieve so much business quickly and turned out to be a billion-dollar company. You can use such strategies for your business as well.

The number three growth hacking strategy can be FOMO. Fear of Missing Out has been of great use in the marketing industry. By creating scarcity about a product or service, there is a high possibility of people ending up buying your product or service or anything you're offering. Showing that only ten quantities or only two consultations are left will help create a scare in your customers' minds and make it look like you're in demand.

The fourth growth hacking technique is called gamification.

"Gamification" can increase traffic to your website. It enhances the user experience and gives a reason for you and your visitors to visit the site. Gamification makes it easy for a business owner to increase the interaction so that they can gain some points or some benefits out of your website. Gamifying the site will not only help the ranking to rise, but also give your user some benefits in the form of points, tokens, or something that they can use elsewhere. Using such techniques will help your visitors interact freely and come again and again for the kind of benefits that they would be getting from the visits. Using gamification has been in play since it increases the value at any time and gives so much importance to the kind of product or service any company would be building.

The fifth strategy could be using a simple footer line. When you're sending out emails, all you have to do is add a hyperlink, which will lead directly to your website or any service that you're providing. The best part about that it leverages the idea that humans are curious beings. Didn't understand? Let me explain how.

Every person is very excited to visit the link that creates curiosity. Adding such a feature can lead to a lot of traffic. Since many people would receive such emails, it can prove to be an excellent marketing strategy.

You know what? Hotmail used this strategy, which helped

them grow to a large number of users in a short period. They grew to 12 million users in their first 18 months that comes to around 20% of the email market then. OptinMonster inspired a small part of this information.

As I repeat in my chapters regularly, all the hacks that I'm giving will help build a business and help increase your brand value. The best part, you can bring a lot of investors on board and generate wealth for all the stakeholders involved.

Growth Hacks for your Business Venture Registering your Business on Google

You can use Google My Business to register your business online so that when your customers search for you on search engines like Google, they can see your profile on the results page itself.

If you search for my business, i.e., Grand Launch on Google, you'll see information on my office, the office timings, ratings on my business, and even a few pictures. When you register with Google My Business, your customers can also find you on Google Maps. Getting yourself a feature on Google Maps will help you get traffic in terms of when people are tagging you on social media. Let's assume you've hosted an event. Your customers can add pictures and videos on social media by tagging you and adding your business location. Such measures help you with organic traffic, and you gain visibility.

Mobile Responsive Website

According to SimilarWeb, in 2017, 63% of site visits were from mobile devices. You need to keep this in mind when preparing for a website. Your website is mostly going to be browsed and visited from mobile phones. Keeping in mind the resolution of a website according to the mobile phone will help your business much more than you think it will. How annoying is it to have a square, stretched out screen of a website and to zoom in a couple of hundred times to take a look at the products.

Enabling a mobile view of your website makes your business appear professional, and obviously, you'll gain traffic since most of the users are using mobiles.

Even portfolio websites are mobile responsive; then an e-commerce should have this feature. If you're getting a new website, which is made totally on a customized basis, you need to get your developer right on track to give you a website that is both mobile and desktop responsive.

Blogs

Having blogs on your website is very important, as this will help you generate SEO-based traffic and give your website visitors a chance to read about your business. You do not necessarily have to just talk about your business. You can talk about other topics related to your industry as well. E.g., If you're into the real estate business, you can write blogs on why you must invest in a house, how a home can be an asset, etc. You can also have blogs that are attached to links that are called backlinks. You can have on-page, off-page SEO done. If you are not aware of SEO in-depth, do not worry. I'll be covering it in the future chapters. How to make your website load faster compared to your competitors? This is the most common problem that every business owner faces nowadays while building a website on their own. First of all, how slow is slow? If your site is not loading in one or two seconds, then it is quiet. A tip with which you can make your site load faster is by compressing all the images and videos and by limiting the unnecessary stuff called plugins that you might have on your website. You can avoid using plugins that delay the launch of your website. This can be in terms of having a WordPress website where only a few plugins are being used in the back end.

Landing Page

The landing page is the first page or the homepage of your website, where clear information about your business is supposed to be given. You also need to add a proper call to action on it. What do you mean by a call to action? A CTA is a small one-liner like Join Now, Learn More, Contact Today, which redirects your visitors to where you want. A proper call to action on your landing page will ensure that your website caters to every possible thing that a visitor is looking for. Your landing page must be simple yet attractive, precise, and have a CTA to capture your visitor's attention. A carefully designed landing page will increase the conversion rate, reduce the bounce rate, and increase the number of emails or the contacts you might collect.

Link your Website

Having a good website means that you need to link that to your social media accounts. You need to have menu options; you need to have About Us, have a homepage, need to have a Contact Us page, and have a presence on many other platforms where you can link it and connect them both. This way, you will have the right presence coming in from different websites and increasing your domain authority. These are the first steps for creating your high ranking SEO website. And linking and connecting this website to different places is very important.

Be Active on Social Media

Social media platforms are known explicitly for getting traffic to your site. When you interact with followers online, you show them that you're not just a brand but also a personality. It's essential to create a figure for your brand. A character similar to your audience will make them want to hang out with you, figuratively, of course. When you share graphics that you know will interest them, they will automatically start sharing them, which will help with engagement. When you post more often, the social media algorithm works for you, making you appear on your follower's feed. This will help you gain organic traffic, get traction, and increase the following that you might learn over time.

Look at what your competitors are doing - Your competitors may have hired digital agency working day and night to increase and generate a lot of traffic for them. You can use similar tactics by spying on your competitors. I'll be talking more about this in the further chapters.

Identifying your USP

As I discussed in the previous sections, your USP is what is going to make you stand out amongst your competition. A USP is not one particular thing. As its name suggests, a Unique

Selling Point can be anything that makes you look unique. It can be your excellent customer service; it can be the difference in your offerings, it can also be in terms of your product where your product offers something more than the competitor's product. You are the best person to identify what that can be. And you're supposed to list them on your website, on your landing page, and also spread the word on social media to let your people and your potential customers know.

Opt-in Page

In simple terms, it's a pop up that appears when someone opens your website. In this pop-up, your users can fill up their details while you can use the same for marketing purposes. This will help you connect with them by using email marketing, SMS marketing, or even the upcoming one, WhatsApp marketing.

Autoresponder on Facebook

You must be living under a rock if you're not familiar with Facebook. There are a lot of tools that can help you add a chatbot system to your Facebook Messenger. The device that I prefer is called Manage Chat. Manage Chat helps me set up different automation and sequencing for my Facebook chat.

Let's take a real-life example. These days, we are hiring a lot of people in digital marketing, and the way I've planned this is as follows. What I do is, I have set an automation system on my manage chat system. That way, I collect automated resumes by sending messages to any person who is chatting with me. They are given an option to select from the menu. The menu option asks if they want to choose my website, they can click on that, apply for jobs, or go towards my online courses. This way, they have an opportunity to choose directly apply for jobs, and an automated message directly goes to them saying that you can send your resume on my so and so email address. This is brilliant because I don't have to monitor my Facebook chat or be active always. Also, it's available 24x7, 365 days, and replies quickly.

Getting your business registered on various website platforms – Let's take an example of Suprcrowd. Suprcrowd, as mentioned in the earlier chapters, is An Automated Affiliate Platform that we, as a company, have launched. It's an e-commerce platform where lots of businesses sell their products and services. When you sell your products on these platforms, firstly, you won't have to worry about marketing since the customers are coming to you directly. You can also generate business since you are allowed to buy, sell, and have a transaction, collect leads, and gain followers on your platform by using An Automated Affiliate Platform.

Digital Agency

When you hire a digital agency, you don't have to worry about marketing. They'll be working to achieve your business goals. The Digital World can be overwhelming, with so many already established platforms to be active on and so many more platforms emerging every day. A digital agency is not just a one or two-person company; it is a combination of 10 to 15 or more people all working to make your marketing best. They work according to your goals and increase the kind of presence that you have ever wanted. And in terms of leading the sales, they will also help you with that.

At Grand Launch, we help our clients gain business in a very sustainable manner. Our clients comprise of clinics, hospitals, educational institutes, cinema halls, malls, clubs, retail showrooms, jewelry industry, education institutes, consisting of preschool, pre-nursery, and much more. With extensive experience, we can cater to all these clients and achieve their revenue targets.

Choose an agency carefully. Choosing them just based on their popularity will do no good if they aren't well-versed with the industry you're in.

Analytics

You need to use proper analytics and tools to identify which platform is giving you more traffic. Let's say you're paying more attention to marketing on Facebook while your customers are mostly coming from Instagram. What a waste of money and effort! Therefore, you must carefully analyze this and market your brand accordingly. Also, with the help of this, you'll get to know more about your target audience.

Decoy Strategy

I'll put this very simply. Have at least three pricing strategies on your website. A Decoy strategy is such that when pricing three types of products, let's assume $10, $15 and $20, they are explicitly defining the gap of $5, $5. But let's assume your pricing is something like $12, $13 and $15. There is a high chance that your customers will go for the $15 item because the kind of value you're providing is much more in the

$15 range. But in the back end, you know that the $10 was supposed to be only $7. You have made your customers think psychologically that the pricing for the $15 is a great deal for them. This way, it will increase your cart value is a great idea and increase your company's revenue in a better manner.

Apple uses this a lot by selling its iPhones in this manner, and you can use that too. Use such strategies to generate more sales with less amount of marketing strategies and ad spend to be done, increasing your ROI in a very positive manner.

The Hidden Psychology to Consumer Marketing

@INCOMEFACT

Small	Medium	Large
$3	$3.50	$3.99

The decoy strategy will make the small and medium items seem overpriced and therefore make it look like the large option is the best deal.

Credits to Incomefact

In comparison to the previous strategies, this is pretty simple.

Use this and boost your Business Growth!

Empowering Quote #8

Only the highly optimized sales funnels will lead to a higher conversion ratio- Shubham Bapna.

Chapter Eight

Spying on your competitors.

I've been mentioning this quite a few times in my book, and I will once again do it. If you want to outstand your competitors, you should know what they're are planning. For that, we must first start by identifying who our competitors are. Then, we will move towards identifying why our competitors are likely to hurt our business in the current scenario. There may be many competitors, but not all of them will be as big as you are in the same playfield. So what do we do? We understand who they are, how they are functioning, how their online digital strategies work like? And the kind of atmosphere

they're working in.

- *We shall also look into understanding the digital strategy that has helped them grow?*

- *What type of SEO keywords they're using?*

- *How much is the traffic on their website?*

- *What is their ranking is in comparison to your website? How much is their market share?*

- *How much is the market share that they're gaining from online marketing?*

This way, we can identify ways in which we will be able to unleash our business online.

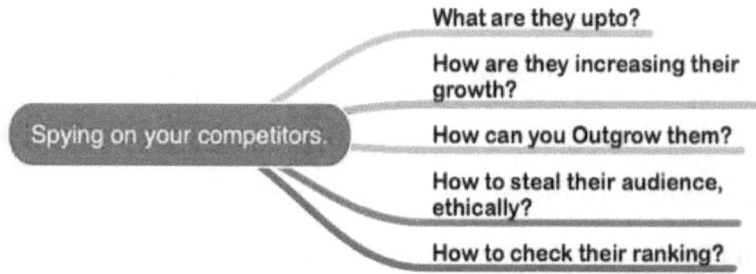

Behind the scenes, Spying on your Competitors

Let's get started.

Competitors are those who are in a similar business as yours. These business owners can either be new or experienced. That honestly does not matter. What matters is that we can get access to all the strategies, keyword, digital footprint, and other data on them if we have the right tools in place. By using tools that are already available in the market, we can identify simply who our competitors are.

○ Step 1:

If you're new to the market and aren't quite aware of who your competitors are, you can use tools like Crunchbase, LinkedIn, or a simple search on Google will also do to identify who the actual players are in the market. Let's get into the details.

○ Are you facing any difficulty finding them? There is a straightforward tool that you can use, called Crunchbase. Crunchbase provides you with a thorough list of your competitors. If you're into a big business, this is a place where you should register yourself.

○ You can also check out Angel.co. Angel.co is another platform for startups, where they can express themselves and check out the kind of tools that they have to search for their competitors and all the other things that you would need to spy on your competitors.

• Step 2:

o The second step is to look into their website and identify how it is structured. You can use tools such as Ubersuggest do that. With the help of these tools, you will be able to identify the traffic, the keywords they're using, etc. SEM Rush, like Uber Suggest, also gives you information on the kind of keywords companies use on their platform in a graphical format.

○ You can also use Gtmetrics, which will help you identify the page load time of your competitor's website. In the previous chapter, I mentioned how important the load time of a page is. This can be one of the things with which you can outdo your competitor. You can identify where they're lacking or what makes them useful. Not just about your competitors, you can also get general information like what page is doing well at the moment, etc.

o   You can also use Google Keyword Planner. It's a superb tool and is free of cost. With this, you don't just get a hold of the general data that other mechanisms are also providing, but you also get to know which kind of path your competitors are taking if they're taking the paid or an organic method.

- Step 3:

You can also use tools such as Spy on Web, which is very popular at the moment by the way, where all you have to do is enter the URL of the website of your competitor and voila! You are introduced to a plethora of information and a detailed analysis of them.

- Step 4:

o   Buzzsumo is also a great website that helps you create viral content. As its name suggests, with its help, you can analyze what content performs best for any topic or competitor. With this tool, you will be able to identify keywords, the kind of hashtags that are trending, and get information on popular influencers.

o Always remember, the trend is your friend. Patterns help you gain massive engagement. Therefore, never underestimate it.

- Step 5:

"Answer the Public" is a website where you can post all your questions related to business. You can post the terms and keywords, which reflect your business. This way, you can identify what kind of tools you will need to grow and what strategies you will need to put your content out there with the help of this tool analyses what kind of questions people ask on the web or social media and present it attractively.

o Let's take an example. If I search for a simple word like "digital" on this platform, it will throw me questions that people have been asking related to that word. "What is digital marketing?" "Which digital camera is good?" "Where is the digital signature used?" "How does a digital piano function?" "What kind of digital strategy should be used?" These are some popular questions that show up if you type "digital." And this is presented in a very systematic manner.

Now with all the advanced tools, we can follow the right

strategies available. Agencies around the world are using this platform to stay up-to-date. Don't miss out. If you make YouTube videos for a living, this platform can be beneficial for you as it helps you understand what kind of content is trending and how you can improve your audience by answering their needs. The next time people search for these questions, they can find your videos or content instead. Using VidiQ for your YouTube video analysis can really bring out the best results.

While using these tools, don't forget to monitor your competitor's website regularly. See how they periodically update it. This will help you understand what they're doing and what makes their website unique - Is it with the help of SEO or with the help of some backlinks that that site must be having? With access to all this data, you can make your strategy that is inspired by them.

Another method to look into what your competitors are up to is by analyzing their social media accounts. When you check out their social media accounts, you'll be able to uncover many things. You can find out what kind of strategies they're following while making graphics, the kind of words, their copywriting, the content, the format, what type of response they're getting from the audience, etc. Above all, are they getting an excellent traction? If yes, then that's what you need to do too.

The Verified Tick

You should also apply for a verified handle. If your business is big enough and has been quickly recognized by many people, you can get your page checked on the social media handles. You will get a blue or a green tick, depending on the kind of platform you're on, signifying that you're a public figure. With a verified social media handle, you will be able to business gain credibility and differentiate you from your competitors. It's essential to figure out which platform you should have your tribe on. Let's say you're into the software business, and if you make an account on Instagram, it won't give you as much benefit compared to if you were on Quora. Your social media accounts should be LinkedIn, Quora, Twitter, and so on. Your competitor will undoubtedly be on these platforms too. You can see how they're functioning, who their followers are, where their followers are from, etc. Then simply use a similar pattern, the same way to reach out to the audience and create a buzz on your product/service or whatever you're offering. This is another method to gain traction and spy on your competitors.

As you might know now, Suprcrowd, our very own Automated Affiliate Platform, also helps identify who your competitors are, what they're doing, and how you can grow beyond them. You can check out the products that they offer, the pricing they go for, and get an overall gist of how their business is working. You can also learn from your competitors' mistakes and make sure you don't repeat them.

Spying Facebook Ads

When you're planning to run your Facebook ads, you can also check out your competitors' ad library. You can come to know what kind of graphics they're adding, what their copies look like, and the type of traffic they're getting from that. Also, see how they're interacting with their audience, see how their audience is responding to them by checking out the comments on their copies. If the audience is liking it, tagging their friends on the comments, it's going well. You'll have an idea of what kind of content your shared target audience wants to digest and what they react to. The next time you make your ads accordingly, you'll gain more control over the market share and have a high return on investment.

Who wouldn't want that?

And it's honestly not as difficult as it looks on paper.

Spying YouTube Channel

Another way to identify your competitor is by simply checking out their YouTube channel, videos, and community. A lot of YouTube videos contain information about the kind of business you're looking for. Let's assume I am looking for competitors in my industry; I would compete with Justdial, Indiamart. Our goal is to take over these platforms in the coming years. There goes a lot of confidence behind saying these things. They are not mear thoughts, but we move with a very structured approach. All the elements have been decided with the help of this book. So here, when I'm absorbing the video content that is being afforded to my customers, I get an idea of what is attracting them, what they're familiar with, and of the planning that my competitors are doing. I'll also know about their new releases and extended features that they're offering in a much better manner since they're explaining in a video.

Spying Influencers

Lastly, you can also check out the influencers or the ambassadors that the company is hiring. This only goes for big companies, though, since not every small business can afford influencer marketing. An ambassador is the face of the product. There's a reason they chose them so carefully. Maybe their personality/lifestyle aligns with the brand.

For eg.,

- Durex will go for Ranveer Singh over any other actor because his fun personality exhibits theirs.

- A fitness brand will go for Shilpa Shetty or any other fitness influencers because

1. Their lifestyle is vibing with their brand ethics

Their audience is similar to the brand's. _Win-Win situation._

These are how you can identify what your competency is up to in a LEGAL way. All these tools are available quickly, and most of them are free too. I would also go out of the way to say that this might act negatively since your competitor also holds the same information on you if they're using these tools. Your competitors can also look into what you're doing, how you're doing, why you're doing, the kind of benefit you're getting, and take advantage of all the things that you are planning to do.

Rest assured, it's a fair-play world, where everyone gets equal opportunities, but what matters is who starts first. The ball is in your court now. I hope you've noted down what all tools you can use and will start working on your strategy accordingly. This is the most crucial way to look into what your competitors are up to. You can find out more information on my website, unleash your business.online/ competitors. This way, we will be updated regularly and can stay in touch with the whole community.

I welcome you with open arms in my Mastermind group, where we learn from each other and grow together, exponentially. The fellow members will help you grow your network, gain more knowledge and ideas, understand how things will work out, and get the best strategies to implement in your business.

That's it for this chapter. Meet you the next.

Empowering Quote #9

Without facts and groundwork, all the digital marketing data is useless- Shubham Bapna.

Chapter Nine

Creating your Sales Funnel

Creating a funnel is by far the most exciting chapter, in my opinion, because I love this topic. Sales Funnel is SO IMPORTANT, and it's almost funny how conveniently businesses seem to ignore and forget this technique. With the help of this technique, you can have control over your customers. Are you now interested? Let's begin.

Imagine a funnel being slit into various parts in a step form. We name this funnel a Sales Funnel. Now let's see what those different parts contain. The steps are as follows -

Lead Generation Lead Nurturing Converting to Sale

Lead Generation is also known as "creating awareness." Naturally, this is the first step in creating awareness and educating your consumers about your product or service with the help of organic or inorganic/paid tools. At this stage, your target audience is strangers to your brand. With the tools' help, you can get an idea of who your potential customers could be. They can provide you with information like the name, mobile number, email address, and so on of your prospect.

Lead Nurturing creates an interest in your potential customer's minds, as they have now considered your brand. This consideration results in them reading reviews on what you offer and trying to understand you. Generation creates intent in the minds of the customers so that curiosity develops. This way, the prospect can make up their mind and turn into a customer by buying your product or service.

Sale, of course, as the name suggests, involves the customer buying what you're selling. Sales mainly involve the financial transaction that takes place at the end of the buying process.

Now that you know what the funnel is like let's dive deep into what makes a funnel a real funnel, and vice versa. We will understand both parts and make sure that we don't make the same mistakes that other people have already made. We will make the best funnels to create content and convert visitors into loyal customers. This is the key to unleashing your business online. Now let's understand why we need sales funnel in the first place. The sales funnel is divided into four simple steps. Four simple steps involve Awareness, Interest, Decision, and Action. When we plan for a sales funnel, we first have to decide what kind of offerings we would provide to our customers or visitors when they visit our website or sales page. The sales page has to be made in a unique manner where the visitor is taken through a dedicated journey. This journey should present the products/services and overall information about your brand in a systematic way.

Then, we need to create interest. Interest can be created in their minds with the help of what's known as social proof. A piece of material evidence, as the name suggests, acts as proof of how the sales have worked so far for the brand. It can be in the manner of testimonials or a social pop-up, etc. This helps generate interest as well as trust and successfully teleports the customers into the Second Stage. Then comes the decision. Will you buy it or not buy it? Our goal is to make them buy, and for that, we will have to trigger something in them so that they move in the right direction. The final step is Action, the moment we've been waiting for, which involves a financial transaction from their end, hence completing the sales funnel.

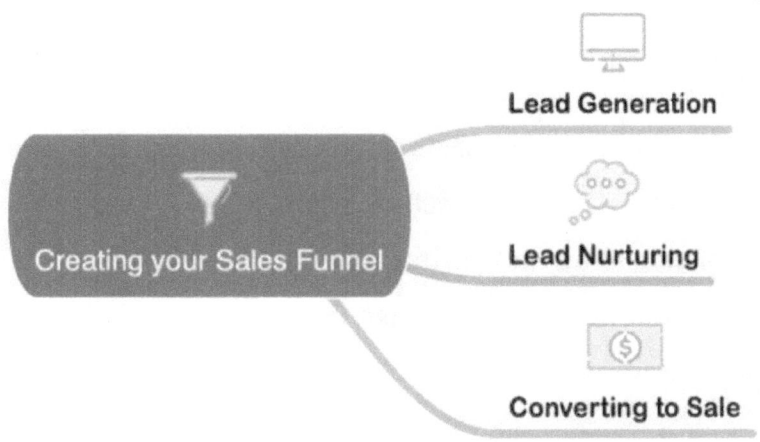

Your Business secret lies here.

An advanced sales funnel takes it one step further. Besides the four levels of awareness, interest, decision, and purchase, there's one more stage: re-purchasing. This stage involves converting one-time customers into loyal customers so that they purchase from you again and again. To ensure that they come back, you have to make sure that you're giving the customer the value that they need. You have to make sure that the customer stays in the loop. Building a relationship with the customers is an integral part of the sales funnel process.

If you want to build the right funnel where you can convert your leads and generate them into massive sales value, you'll need to follow specific steps. These steps inherently involve three things – High Converting landing pages are developed. It must provide a clear understanding of your offerings and must have social proof.

Highly automated email marketing system. Automated SMS

To complete the last two steps, you must make sure that they're not leaving your website without giving their personal information. You need to set up a system that collects their contact information on the page. See, the idea behind this is straightforward. You're spending so much on ads to make a mere prospect a visitor. You can't afford to let them go away without giving you something in exchange. Even if it's not a financial transaction, it should at least be valuable information, i.e., their details. At least you can work with that. This stage is critical.

Now, since I've given you an overview of how funnels work, let's dive into building a sales funnel and how to do it systematically.

Step one

Build a website. Having a site that has a brilliant landing page will act as the first and the necessary level of a funnel. Let's take up a quick example of this book itself, for this step. I will be doing this practice and showing you how I will sell my book using the same method I'm talking about. If you visit my website, www.unleashyourbusiness.online, you will be able to see the exact funnel. If you don't read this chapter, you will think it's an essential website. But if you have an idea of how to identify a funnel and locate it, and what are the steps, and automation that is happening behind the scenes, you can see the magic and will be able to appreciate the kind of efforts that go into making a high funnel.

Before we get into the depth and the steps of making a funnel, I would like to present you with a brilliant opportunity. If you just study this particular chapter, you will be able to take away the skills and perhaps, even freelance and charge other business people by making funnels and helping them generate revenue that they hadn't even thought of. It's a great business opportunity that you can implement in your as well as a client's business. This way, you can increase so much value of your and your client's account.

When you're planning to build a brilliant funnel, you need to identify the business model. If I'm planning to get a website, what do I expect this website to do for me? If my expectation is just to collect leads, then I'll be focusing on a lead generation-based funnel. If my focus is on selling something, my planning will be surrounded by the process leading to the creation of a sales-based funnel system. So, first things first, identify what the outcome expected out of this funnel system is. The remaining items can change accordingly. What is the result that you want to achieve when you're building this website? Whether it is to sell information or products, gather data via lead generation, or perhaps even gift something free to your clients. Always remember that in return, you must be able to get information about your prospects. This step also helps in building your business story.

Step two

It is all about having the right tools in place to make your website. You need to use the right tools because building a website containing your whole funnel will be complicated without them. You can go for various devices such as Click Funnels, Igloo, Elementor, and many other available themes.

Your goal is to optimize and use the best possible tool that fits your budget. If you go for Click Funnels, then the cost starts from around $99 per month and upwards. If you are a person who is just beginning and can't invest so much at once, there are even a few affordable and free tools that are available. Igloo and Elementor come at a reasonable price compared to Click Funnels. Igloo is a great app that helps you build mind-blowing landing pages. I, myself, use Igloo and am a big fan. I have bought a lifetime deal, which is very economical. With their unconditional offer, I can make myself as many pages as I want to and build a high funnel. After completing the first two steps, which is website building, I brisk towards finding a platform where I can host this very website. I use my private servers for my business, but I can recommend Hostgator, Bluehost, or even GoDaddy. GoDaddy is a little complex compared to the other two. In my view, Hostgator gives the best deals. It is recommended for beginners.

To sum it up, we're building a website with the best tools and a host that provides an economic platform.

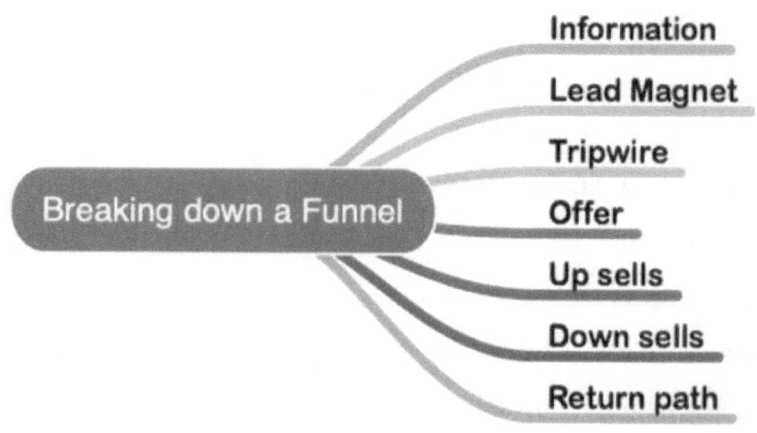

Crucial Funnel terminologies What makes a funnel?

A funnel consists of - Information, Lead Magnet, Tripwire, Offer, Upsells, Downsells, Return path, and much more. And mind you, these are just the necessary steps that are a part of an even bigger funnel system. Here is what happens, when you want to collect any lead or information from someone, you have to offer them something in return, right? When you visit my website, unleashyourbusiness.online, you find a simple link that enables you to download a free copy of the first chapter of my book. But in return, you must provide your contact information.

Since you're downloading that information, you're downloading a PDF, which will be sent to you directly by my autoresponder. This autoresponder is an email marketing software that runs behind the scenes when anyone reaches the landing page. Also, let me tell you, this landing page for giving away my free eBook is made on lead pages.

The first page is another software with which I can directly connect my domain with the platform I bought, like GoDaddy or Namecheap. I can change a few settings in the DNS, get my website on lead pages, and build a great landing page. Superfast, super-efficient. I don't need to have any hosting platform because that's what lead pages do. It helps you create a trade website without having a hosting platform, and I've used the same for my www.unleashyourbusiness.online free lead magnet copy.

When people visit the aforementioned landing page, they understand what I'm offering, and the benefits of this book, and getting a free copy in return for their information. This information is valuable since it helps me build a database. A database of potential customers can help email them. An email will help me in marketing my book. This way, I can strike up a conversation or start sending them emails to cross-sell or even upsell them in terms of different offerings that I might have.

So, the moment they give me their name, mobile number, and email ID, I send them an automated email along with the PDF copy of my first chapter. They can read the section and ultimately decide whether to buy it or not. This builds trust and credibility in the subscribers' eyes as I've sent them what they wanted as promised—letting you in on a secret. You see, the customers think you're taking their information to send them that copy while you're using it for a much bigger purpose. This is very helpful and acts as a great lead magnet, where you're providing something to your customers or even visitors and earning a place of trust in their minds. This will help you build your database and give you a potential list of active participants in your business journey.

Then comes the second step in the core part of funnels, called creating an offer and going for the tripwire. I'll be leaving a simple, but handy funnel diagram right here to look into it and understand how a simple funnel is planned out. This might sound really out of the world or even tough to understand, but once you get the hang of the art of creating a funnel, you will fall in love with it and implement it everywhere in your life. That's my bet. Whether you're talking to your girlfriend, selling online, or offline, this is being used everywhere in all possible conversations and deals you may have ever encountered. You wouldn't have recognized it at first, but now that you'll know, you'll know. You'll reap great benefits once you start applying this online. With the help of the tools that I'll show you, you can start building your funnel system right from the moment you complete this chapter.

Coming back to the tripwire and the offer that we are going to create, let me first start by asking - Why do we need to create a proposal?

After all, an offer or a tripwire is a low-value item. It's a low-cost offering you give to your customers temporarily so that they don't perceive you as too expensive. Once you start offering them some cheap products or low-ticket items, they wouldn't mind purchasing them from you after that as well. What is the result of this? You get to convert these buyers into real customers. When they buy these offerings from you, they don't feel the pinch of it being a very high-value product. This tripwire offering can be in terms of the price range, which falls between Rs. Five hundred to even 5000 rupees. If you convert this into dollars, it would be around $10 to anything between $80 - $90. Here, no one would mind paying something in such a small amount when you're providing a massive value. Massive value is the key to success when attracting people to take active participation in the funds that you're building. When people start joining and showing interest in you, lure them with these offers to get converted into customers.

Let's continue with the example of my website for this book. So far, you went through my website, signed up for the first chapter, and received that via email while I've got your contact in my database in return. Now let's say you found it interesting and decided to buy it. You go back to my website and order the book. Now, this is where my funnel system starts. When you come to my website to purchase the magazine, you come across another offer for an online course. This book acts as a tripwire, and the previous PDF copy acts as a lead magnet. As I mentioned earlier, a tripwire offer is priced around 500 to 5000 rupees, and this book is valued at $4.99, i.e., one rupee shy of 500 rupees, which to be honest isn't of much value to me. Once you're into my funnel system where you've already purchased the book, I come up to you with another valuable product, i.e., my online course.

This online course is about unleashing your business online in a video format. Everyone loves to read, but learning something from a video format helps you understand and picture the flow better. This video format is priced at a certain amount of rupees that I will soon be releasing on my coaching platform. Unleash your online business course will help you understand this concept in depth with me, I'll be posting recorded sessions of how I build things from start to end, everything from scratch.

Since I've provided you with a lead magnet and a tripwire offer, now I go ahead with a bump offer. A bump offer is when I combine with my previous suggestion, i.e., my book, an additional offer, i.e., the online course. I hide the actual price of the product and, instead, conclude it with a rate that appears to be more affordable since it is offering two things. This combined offer will help you understand and make sense of my concepts better. And if you look at it from a seller's point of view, the seller receives much more than what they would get with the tripwire item.

This strategy has been practiced for ages by so many well-known business houses. When you go to the mall, they entice you to visit their showroom and look into their product section by offering you their lowest ticket item. And just when you're thinking of buying it, they offer you an upgrade, i.e., they show you another offer and ask if you would want it to be combined with the previous item.

So the next time you visit a mall and witness the same moment, remember that this is what is called a Bump. A bump, as the name suggests, is a little hike in the product value and the total cart value leading to a higher conversion rate for the seller. And now you can use the same strategy for various offers too.

If you're wondering why I'm telling you about the strategies that I used for the book, let me tell you that I am sincere and always give my best to people. Always happy to be providing you with massive value. Trust me when I say this when you're able to apply the various information and strategies I've been churning out throughout the book, into your business in a real sense. My level of happiness would be so much more than the mere feeling of insecurity for sharing my secrets.

Now that we've completed the bump offer, I'll show how we can execute, down sells, bring them back to our funnel journey, and provide them with some other products with the help of the same system.

Welcome to Part 2 of Funnels, where we'll be learning in great detail about upsells and downsells. Behold! We're not done with the offers just yet. Upsells are something that I'm going to be providing apart from the primary offering that I did in the first part. Here, when the visitor comes through my autoresponder. (If you remember the autoresponder part, then you will know what software I'm talking about. Let me give you a hint. This software helps me automate my email marketing system. Any clue?)

Drumrolls...

ConvertKit! As I mentioned in the earlier chapters, ConvertKit helped me automate my system, which helped me in targeting my customers a whole lot better and in a very systematic manner. This also gave me a lot of confidence while I was scaling my business, you see, you can't just sit and type each email manually, esp. when you're thinking of scaling your business. While it's the whole system of taking a business online, the fundamentals and the pros of taking your business online are that you can automate your entire digital journey by using the right tools in the proper sense.

Simply put, the act of offering something more to your existing customers is known as an upsell. Upsell is different, though, from what I provided earlier. Have you ever shopped on

Amazon? If not, check now. When you click on the product you like, and as you scroll down to click the purchase option, you come across a recommendation list, don't you? And in that recommendation list, you see another item beside it.

You start thinking of buying it. Together, it is labeled as "Frequently bought together," basically telling you that other users have purchased the topic of your interest along with these additional items. That means that this is something that they are providing you over and above your actual offering. This is called a bump offer again, but if you look closely, you will realize that they're just upselling you below that. When they upsell you something that is over and above the tripwire and the bump offer, it means that they're selling you 5X the original tripwire offer.

Another thing they do is, offer you a membership, an Amazon Prime membership, an Amazon Kindle membership or any other offers that are going around in that period. But they're just upselling you and showing you that even these could be the possible purchases you can make. You get more value; they get more dollars. And their profit doesn't stop there. If you think about it, their cart value increases, and their sales volumes increase, and they can sell more without the additional cost of marketing each of their services all over again, thus improving their final ROI.

In any kind of business, marketing is always considered an investment. Once you find it as an investment, then only will you start visualizing a clear roadmap towards your return on investment journey. Always remember this point because this forms the crux of online marketing. Since we're providing some upsells to our existing customers, I'll be bringing you back to the original example, i.e., my website, unleashyourbusiness.online. Since the basic offer has already been provided, and I'll continue to build trust among my existing customers through email marketing, my next step will be to offer another book, like Part 2. This book, though mostly about the online world, will be a different topic.

Let's say the offer is "Grand Launch Academy Mastermind membership". This offer will be different from my original proposal, and with this offer, I can help them learn and understand things in a very different manner. With this book, I'll be able to teach them X, Y, and Z things. These things will be listed on my funnel page. I will have to follow the same steps all over again and build the same funnel for this product. When I start building the funnel for this product, I'll also be creating something known as a downsell.

Let's assume I'm giving this book for around $9.99; I can offer them a downsell item in the form of an Ebook. An ebook could be something of approximately four double lines, five double lines, or even lower than the actual book. The idea behind this is that since this book/hard copy is more expensive, there is a chance of customers declining it, but when you introduce an alternative product for a lower price, they might just consider it. And the best part is – Since they are existing customers, they're likely to go for the hardcopy anyway. Therefore, I need to keep the offer, so people go forward and buy the book's actual hard copy. When they go for the hard copy, it helps me increase my cart value. Even the customers, they'll be getting a real book rather than a PDF copy, something that will just lie on their computer after a point without having the chance to be ever opened again. This is down selling.

One last thing I wanted to cover is what I call the Return Path. When you're using automation software like Pabbly Connect, and other tools that help you do the same, connect these different applications to make your life simpler. For this, you need to create a return path. The return path is when I'm giving my autoresponder and my automation tool the authority to, let's say, if the user purchases my book, then send them a soft copy directly. Similarly, if this user decides to buy the hard copy, your system must, on its own, find it out. It can then instruct the logistic partners to collect the book from the warehouse and deliver it at the said location—all of this occurring without you having to move an inch away from your chair.

Integrating applications play a significant role here.

Everything will be streamlined in such a brilliant manner.

Now you might say, "Shubham, reading about creating a funnel strategy and implementing it in business are two very different things." For all those saying that I suggest you go through my website and check out my online course. See, I do not deny that it will be difficult. Of course, theories and practices are different. And that's precisely why I've created the online course. With the online course, you'll see how a strategy is executed systematically; you'll be able to participate in active discussions and ask me your doubts directly since I'll also be going live. You can get practical knowledge of what we're teaching here now. You will also get a chance to join Grand Launch Academy, where we connect, network, strategize, and brainstorm together. We've covered a lot of different strategies already and will be covering even more, but for now, I will come back to the tools that we will be used to create excellent funnels.

Let's talk about finance. While creating a funnel of your own, you will need a fund of at least $1,000. Having 60,000 rupees to 70,000 rupees in your bank will help you carry these tools over five to six months sustainably. I won't give you any false promises, but building such funnels requires you to buy some fantastic tools. By that I mean, don't just go for the free products because lets be honest, free things are not valued much. They don't provide you with as many inputs as they would with a paid plan. And when you start paying for good things, they give you a return in value over time.

Remember I touched upon the various applications you'll need to make a website and how Click Funnels is much more expensive than the rest, I would like to add that Click Funnels gives you the added benefits they charge way too much for them. If you still want to go for it, I suggest you go for the $99 per month package to automate your whole process and make it easier for you to create a sales funnel. The kind of email software that you would need where it works is an autoresponder. This autoresponder will help you target your customers, and leads, and send them all the required information to build a tremendous conversational email. This will be done with the help of ConvertKit. ConvertKit is a paid application, but it's the most effective one out there. It helps you send massive amounts of emails with different pricing limits over the number of subscribers that you would be having.

Once you have these things in place, you can start using the different payment gateways. I would suggest you either go for Razorpay or Recipe. If you're in India, you can access these easily. If not, you can also go to Stripe. Stripe offers excellent solutions for your business payment gateway where you can collect fees, your costs amount, business transactions, and more.

Lastly, we can connect all these applications with another application called Pabbly Connect.

Pabbly Connect helps me combine webhooks to automate all these zaps, sending automated SMS, all of this while building a great relationship with all my customers. All this may be overbearing to register right now, but trust me, once you give this a go, your whole journey will be extraordinarily seamless and transparent. The entire idea behind this process is to automate your digital business. And another thing that you would gain from here is the possibility of unleashing your business online. This has to be the most exciting topic as this is the practical part of getting down and understanding all that we've learned in the last eight chapters and implementing them into our funnel. And building a website, and creating a high funnel is the necessary foundation through which your online business can go to the next level. Keeping these steps in mind and keeping a systematic plan in place will help you create the foundation right. Get the basics done, and allow yourself to create a high sales funnel with the help of all the digital automation software that I've mentioned above.

If you have any doubts or want to learn more about funnels, you are always welcome to our online course available on unleash your business.online. We all know how COVID rolled out, and I don't want to bring the quarantine flashbacks back.

But we can't hide from the fact that it has affected the business world in more ways than others. I wouldn't even be surprised to know if you picked up this book solely because of the COVID repercussions and how it has forced everybody to go online. Keeping all this in mind, I know how nerve-racking it is to think about how the post-COVID world will be. Our online course will cover all of this in great detail, so do not worry.

Having said all this, let me end this on a good note. I'm so glad you finally chose to take the path up the digital world, the way toward the future.

I'll see you in the next chapter; it's all about promotion offers - Cannot be Ignored.

Empowering Quote #10

People don't buy what you do; they buy why you do it- Shubham Bapna

Chapter Ten

Promotion Offers that can't be ignored

Since we've gone through understanding the mindset possibilities, analyzing your business, creating a business story, identifying the right strategies, letting alone growth hacks, spying on your competitors, and creating your sales funnel, we move towards integrating promotion offers. Let's start with how we can develop such suggestions and pricing strategies. We'll understand what kind of numbers we'll have to use so that the customer or the prospect will most likely be encouraged to purchase the offering that you're providing. We will be going through this in detail, so stay on your toes and make sure that you are implementing all of these in your business because reading them will only give you knowledge, not results. Applying them to your business or your client's business will help you come at a clear growth strategy to unleash your business online. Let's get started.

This is a significant chapter, and you'll get a lot to learn from this. I'll be teaching you how to create amazing promotions with great pricing, great strategies, and a lot of effort so that they can be generated, and your hard work will pay off successfully.

Number one way to create amazing offers that your visitors can't ignore, no matter what they are.

Gamification

You can use gamification as a technique by creating artificial scarcity for your products if you're dealing with e-commerce. If you have an e-commerce platform, you can show a limited quantity of your product and services to look like it's something urgent to invest in. It doesn't matter if you have an unlimited number; if you show a limit, the customers wouldn't even think twice before buying your offerings. So don't worry; this is a legit business; every e-commerce platform uses this technique. All you're doing is limiting the offerings to your public.

Much like window shopping, viewers also like to go

through the website just to pass their time. There is a natural reluctance in their behavior that does not let them shop even if they badly want that product. All of us have that in us somewhere we like to push things until it's urgent. Taking this customer behavior into the note, all I'm saying is to show urgency so that it triggers the impulse in them. Your products will be sold out in no time.

Let's assume that you're running a webinar online, and there is a web page that leads you to register for the webinar. If you've ever attended a webinar, you might have seen that they almost always offer limited seats. This is to show the user that 1. It's urgent; you'll be left out if you don't hurry; 2. Many people are interested, and the seats are packed in no time. You tend to register quickly due to this. One more advantage of this is that only affected people will show up; this means that you now know who your target audience is and can continue to contact them. Try this method of having a limited plan; it's beneficial.

Now let's say you're experiencing cross-sells. You're providing a service, which is linked to another facility in some different offering, and let's assume you have planned for offers A and B to be combined. If you use the same funda and run a promotion that has a limited period, you'll trigger a response in your users. They'll see that there's a limit and quickly pounce on the offer.

And if they don't understand and buy the offer, they will miss out on the great deal that could have happened.

Let's assume that you're booking an online ticket for traveling from point A to point B. This will need you to not only arrange for flight tickets, but you'll also have to book hotels and let's say car rentals. If you've ever planned travel, you'll be familiar with this. Of course, they can't put a limit on places, but what they can do, though, is set a limit on time. So what they do is, tell the customers that the offer is valid till a specific time, which results in people almost always taking up the offer due to excitement. Sometimes they even book things that they don't need. This kind of promotion offer works well and helps increase cart value.

We are not going into the right or wrong part because our topic is unleashing your business online. You can use any strategy, be it right or wrong, find the ethical role, and customize it accordingly. These strategies are all available, you just need to have a keen eye to look into these strategies and understand them, how they function, how they work, and how the flow is, and you can use the same in your business. The only thing you need to learn is the ability to spot them. As you go through the chapters, you'll automatically sync it into that thought process and start placing ideas and offers seamlessly.

Coupons

Coupons or discounts with running time are what we've all witnessed in our buyer's journey. And we all know it works quite well too. Companies usually sell all their outdated products and clear their inventory for more replenishment during such sales. We also call it the "Clearance Sale." When you're having more stock coming in, your sales, your turnover, and all the ratios will turn positive. And this will not only help you increase your business but will also increase the revenue per customer, and over some time, your sales will turn out to be high compared to what the other customers would be facing with different buyers. As a buyer, every customer wants more and more offers. When they find a seller giving such suggestions regularly, they are more likely to stay loyal customers. Always remember to provide some discounts from time to time. This creates something that every company looks forward to – Word-of-Mouth marketing. We all know how effective that is.

There is also a possibility of having a live chat engagement when you're chatting live online on the website or a chatbot. This will improve your conversion rates. Customers with doubts can use the chatbox and have a conversation with the seller; they can also discuss what kind of offers are going on. Even the seller can collect some information about the buyer and reach out to them next time, thus putting them in the funnel loop.

Another promotion offers could be created by providing some recommendations that are based on personal behavior. This involves many algorithms and sophisticated features that will need to be adjusted in your eCommerce platform. Using SaaS platforms like Shopify or Bigcommerce will help you in such situations in terms of identifying the buying pattern of every user and how similar they are to one another. And once this platform trains itself, it becomes straightforward and useful when scaling your business according to the personal needs of the visitors visiting your platform. A seller needs to understand that regular stock should be updated in terms of the high-moving items. In the customer's eyes, it will look like your products are always available, which will improve your credibility and sales.

Influencer Marketing

Now coming to perhaps the most awaited offer, something that almost every brand is using right now is the Influencer Marketing technique. Using influencers to brand and market your products will help both ways, they get a commission or free offerings, and you grow organically. Nowadays, customers are more likely to purchase products from influencers whom they trust, and whom they idolize and respect on social media. You won't believe these influencers have even higher convincing power compared to hefty paid celebrities. The best part about this is that you don't have to go looking for your target audience since they already have access to them and can talk to them directly. Such influencers could work for you for any business at a very nominal cost and give you a high ROI in terms of the branding that needs to be done.

Hashtag marketing.

You can also do hashtag marketing by merely creating a unique, catchy, and separate hashtag just for your business. These hashtags can be used by your customers, past customers, influencers, etc., too, when they want to post something about you. An added benefit of this is that it can also act like a data storage kind of thing, which means that you can access it and see who all have used it over time.

People tend to believe in anything, even bullshit, for that matter if repeated multiple times. You can use this psychology trick to your advantage by appearing in front of them numerous times. You can do this with hashtags. When there is an increase in the frequency of the hashtags, and people see it everywhere, of course, curiosity will be generated, and people will consider looking into you. This works well because it's subtle too. Ultimately, no matter how good your products and services are, the world is more or less brand-crazy. Therefore brand visibility for any brand in any sector is necessary.

You can also use different strategies and customize your checkout page. The checkout page is where you're having different currencies being lifted out, depending on the visitor's IP. Let's assume that your business is located in Hong Kong, and that your customer is based in the UK. You can have a system on your platform, which automatically converts the Hong Kong dollars option into Great Britain Pounds. The conversion of the value of the currency will also be done. One more trick that you can use is converting the sold products' rate into the local currency so that you look global as well as regional at the same time. "Glocal," as the new term goes, will help you gain a better reputation and offers compared to your competitors. In case they're just focusing on the local currency, you can go for minimal customizations, which will help you out in creating better promotion offers for anyone visiting your website from any possible country. And thus, there is a high possibility of increasing sales. Now you have an opportunity to give your best products and services to the world at great pricing.

Another great way of promoting offers that cannot be ignored is by giving away loyalty and referral points. When you give loyalty or referral points to the buyers or even create an affiliate platform on your website, you encourage your visitors to take participate in this program. All they have to do is promote your products and get a commission in return. This way, both the parties involved earning.

Giveaways

Another way to create amazing offers for your visitors and at the same time, make your offerings go viral is by using Giveaways. Giveaways develop a sense of urgency and a sense of FOMO. If you're not millennial enough, let me jog you through this. It's the Fear of Missing Out, which is a feeling you get when everyone around you participates in a trend, and you feel like you're obligated to do the same. FOMO acts as a trigger, which encourages your customers to buy products and services from your website. This can also result in the awakening of flash sales on your platform. You must have heard about flash sales. Flash sales are nothing but offers that runs on limited products with minimal quantity, and they have a limitation on time too. Best of three worlds. You must have experienced or at least witnessed it at some point, probably while buying, like, mobile phones on Amazon or Flipkart. I purposely used this example as this sale works best on mobile phones, in my opinion. Phones get sold within a minute. Thousands and thousands of phones are sold like this, and the kind of transactions that happen really can only be dreamt of.

FOMO

You can use a similar technique on your business website by creating FOMO. Create fear in the customers' minds, which will encourage them to purchase your products/services as quickly as possible. This will increase your revenue drastically.

You should also master the art of using colors smartly to attract users to click on them. Usually, most "click here" buttons come with the color green because green stands for growth and money. People typically have a positive outlook toward this color.

As for the color red, the red button is something that transmits a lot of energy, as well as shows that there could be a possibility of danger. Therefore, use this color with caution. You can use this color when you're giving offers as this color stands out and attracts attention. Make sure that your promotional offers are useful in terms of copywriting, but also have the right combination of colors, which will help them gain better traction, and the chance of users clicking on them is high.

You can also give your visitors some lead magnets, as we discussed in the previous chapter. Lead magnets help you achieve the first step of the funnel, and promoting such offers could be helpful for your business. You can give some time offers where you're offering a sale for a certain period, and they need to address specific criteria. Having criteria in mind will not only target the real potential customers but also filter out and avoid getting any cart abandonment.

Cart abandonment

Cart abandonment usually occurs when the checkout platform or even the offers that were previously shown to the visitors was something different and varying from the ads that were shown during the promotion. Hence, your ads and website information should always be in sync. It should be aligned. There should not be any misleading information because misleading information will result in a lack of trust and a lot of dollars, which could have been avoided if things were portrayed honestly. You can also collaborate with different platforms giving a combination of offers. You could provide them with bonus cards, Groupon, coupons, or even some different offerings from other companies altogether. This collaborative offer could result in a great promotion, thereby creating an interest in the visitor's mind as this is not something that is witnessed every time. Such platforms are needed to bring out the best offers. Having such offers to attract new customers leads to viral marketing. The affiliate army will help you get a lot of customer base in return for some commission, which could boost social sharing.

One of the best ways to increase your sales is by providing discounts. Discounts are the oldest techniques out of the lot, which to date works in a very positive manner by giving limited-time discounts to your visitors. This also helps increase the time they spend on the website to understand the intent behind the offering that you're providing them. Providing pop-ups for such discounts on your landing page will increase your chances of on-the-spot conversions. You can also use different pop-up companies such as m OptinMonster, Trustpulse, Sumo, Bloom, or Thriveleads.

Free shipping

You can also provide free shipping. People love free shipping. The word "Free" is itself so enticing, and it's all the more exciting if this word is used for transportation. Shipping costs a lot, and this helps the customers save a lot. They'll appreciate this effort. And don't worry, you won't miss out on a penny. All you have to do is add the money that goes into the shipping to the value of your product. It's a gimmick, I agree. But almost every company uses this. It's up to you whether to choose this or not.

Okay, let's assume you're selling something for around

$100, but the shipping cost is about $105. Yes, it can get that expensive. You plan on giving a discount of 10%. The pricing could be as follows. You will price it at $100 and provide $5 on the shipping, so that comes to around $105, now give a discount by reducing the amount by $10 on the base price which comes to $90. And $90 plus $5 shipping, comes to around

$95. Now all you have to do is tell your customers that you're covering the entire shipping cost.

On top of that, they're even getting a discount, an exclusive discount of 5%. There, you just created a super attractive offer. This information can bring in a lot of sales when you combine many other proposals, forming a whole funnel structure. You can have various deals coming up on different, different days, such as Black Friday, Good Friday, Christmas, Happy New Year deals, and so many out there.

These are some fantastic ways in which you can plan out amazing deals that will profit both your and your customers. You can also use Facebook ads, Instagram, Twitter, LinkedIn, Quora, YouTube, Google AdWords, and many other ad platforms. To smartly place your ads everywhere and increase your reach, traffic on the website, and conversion rate will eventually lead to a massive increase in sales. You're nurturing these offers with the help of all the possible tools that I mentioned in the previous chapters. If this speedy approach keeps going, you will be able to create a high sales funnel with a proper promotion strategy.

Empowering Quote #11

Digital Marketing is an Investment.

Considering it as an expense can break your Business- Shubham Bapna.

Chapter Eleven

How to win Clients before selling them

Selling to your clients is very easy if you have a great offering in place. Let's assume the offering that you're providing is

not that great, but you still want to sell to your customers, what you need to do is place something on the pricing part. But in case you're not able to find some gaps in the pricing and give your customers a reasonable discount offer, what you can do is provide some value-added services so that the offering looks so attractive that you don't have to sell them at all. Don't worry; we will be breaking down various techniques with the help of case studies. We will understand how we can win the clients before even selling to them.

All right, so before getting into the customer's deep psychology to win them over, we need to understand the different avenues where we can win the clients and the platforms where we can use such promotion techniques. Thanks to digital marketing and social media tools, it is straightforward to reach out to multiple groups and inform about your offering to numerous people without even being in direct contact with them. Yes, I'm talking about winning clients over through influencers and celebrities. Customers tend to trust their favorite influencers a lot, and their fantastic way of marketing adds a bonus. The customers will be rushing toward the payment gateway in no time. You won't believe the influencer's power is such that some fans would even pay any amount for the product just because they recommended them. Ultimately it's your offering that's going to make them stay. Therefore, you need to balance both of these things and make sure that there is no such thing available in the market that can replace the offering that you're providing.

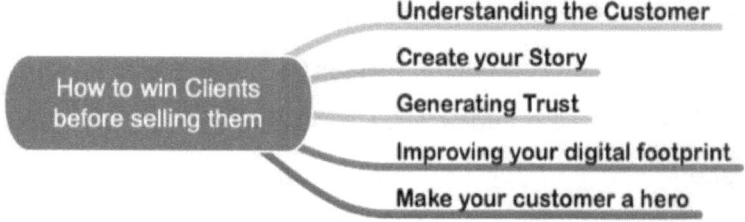

Win clients and turn them into your Loyal Sales Army Let's imagine that the kind of product you're offering to the public is already available in the market. This will create some differences in the pricing. This will even bring down your sales because a competitor is offering the same product. There are possibilities that your customers can go to the competitors. There is also a high possibility that your conversions will fall. Your translations are about how unique your product is. The USPs matter a lot, the kind of branding, features, and understanding of the market and your customers is essential.

Once you start systematically understanding all these things, you will be able to offer your clients and customers exactly what they need. And if there's no competitor at the moment, even better. But don't be too happy too soon. As a business that arrived at the market first, you do have a first-mover advantage, but you need to understand that in the end, you can't control your customers and that they have the power to dissuade. Therefore, you must be prepared for the worst and start bringing in loyalty programs early on before the unnamed happens.

One more important topic that we must cover is how to get your customers to talk about your business without you having to persuade them. This is way different from the Affiliate marketing program as this does not involve you paying them. They do it willingly. One of the best ways to execute this is by getting into a partnership with something that connects your business to them. Another way in which you can win your future customers is by showing them how much you care about the world and also their feelings. You can post about LGBT on your social media handles, or talk about other social issues that you support. In case you're into sports apparel, you can sponsor and support your favorite sports stars. You can also conduct contests and giveaways as they create curiosity and excitement and, again, prove to be a proper marketing technique. A lot of business owners I know are using such methods to develop interest, generate traffic, and ensure that the brand is always alive.

For keeping the brand alive, you need to hire a person, a person who could be a face or the brand ambassador of your offerings. Once you have the brand ambassador in place, brand recognition will be easy as the audience is already familiar with your brand's face. Additionally, it's not just them as the face, but their personality also massively influences your brand. Therefore, while choosing a brand ambassador, make sure that their persona aligns with yours.

Is it possible to win a customer even before selling it to them? Yes, it is. That's where the lead magnet comes to play. The lead magnet will help bring the customers to you. Still, after that, it's up to you to nurture them, keep them interested, send emails regularly or conduct seminars or be active on social media, etc.

"This world can become exceedingly successful and exceedingly useful."

Mr. Peter Drucker coined this term. Peter Drucker, as you know, is the king of marketing. And along with the numerous books he has written over the years, he has also managed to pass down an overload of information to the world, which genuinely translates into creating trust in this person. This is a great way to create a brand, as well. You can use similar patterns, similar strategies, and apply them to your business. As I mentioned in the first line of this chapter, selling your product is easy. It's the trust part that you must conquer. You can do that by giving away your products for free or for a trial to make sure that they trust the product first, and then purchase the offering that you're preparing for them.

How can you use a digital platform for the same purpose of creating trust? One possible way is by using automated webinars. You can record a session and run a computerized webinar, which will then be run using promotions and campaigns. Such campaigns could bring a lot of leads to your website and encourage them to register for the pre-recorded webinar. Using a proper funnel system, as discussed earlier, you can help them to record, and once they register, you can take them to a separate webinar room. This webinar room will be all about promoting your product, features, services, offers, and a payment gateway link will also be attached at the end. You can also automate this whole digital journey.

Once you start doing that and eventually start scaling, there is a high possibility that a lot of customers will be more than happy to try out the product or service you're providing. They may even ask more about the offer just by taking a glimpse of the whole structure of how you have presented the webinar. You can use NLP and other fantastic tools that help you market to your customers with credibility and help you structure the words and the sales pitch correctly. In such a way that will inevitably lead to higher conversions regarding the ad spend you're making.

Why do I keep repeating ad spend, ROI, and higher results at the end of every explanation? When you're doing your business online, it is essential to look at the metrics. Since the ad spends are intangible and will only show you the results over time, you won't even understand when you've destroyed your budget. You will only realize it when you don't have any more money to spend. Ad spends no joke and, if executed in the wrong way, can be very heavy on your pockets. Therefore, it's essential to understand the concepts thoroughly and then decide the kind of strategies you'll be using to implement in your online business.

Another way to create credibility in the eyes of new customers is by using a referral system. Using the referral and testimonial technique brings in the trust factor even without them trying your offering. Creating trust in the minds of a visitor or your potential customer is the most critical part of any business and should be performed to perfection. What is the first thing you look for when you're shopping online? What are the points that you would charge a website or a company for? Is the company even well-known? The company has to be well known because only then would people be more excited about buying from them. If your company is not that known or new, you need to create social trust. And for that, you must invest in testimonials or encourage reviews. And to answer the question I asked before, this is the first thing people look for while shopping online.

Let's take an example from my book. There may be a chance that you might have purchased my book after reading a review, and that says a lot. Even if this didn't happen, let me give you a glimpse of the power of testimonials. Many eminent personalities have given their testimonials and spoken to me. They talked about who I am, what I do, what qualities I possess, and how this book can bring out the best in them. This will impact my books for years to come, as the feedback accumulates, and eventually, the word-of-mouth game picks up. And when that happens, we use that as an advantage to launch another book, part 2 of this book, Scaling Your Business Online. Yes, yes, I have planned well ahead already.

Now, how am I creating social trust about this book, about me, and all the things that are working in sync to make this book a success? If you type my name on Google or any other search engine for that matter, you'll see that the first five pages will be about me. There is only one Shubham Bapna, according to Google, and it's because, over the years, I have built multiple links on multiple channels, platforms, and websites, basically making an online presence. I'm also known on social media by the name of 10X Shubhan Bapna. When I keep myself out there by having my videos on YouTube, by having my podcast on Spotify, Apple, Google, and so many other platforms, I create a lot of social and digital footprints.

This digital footprint is beneficial for any visitor checking out the credibility of my offering. It takes a lot of time to build social credibility and a digital print, but you need to start now so that over some time when things start accumulating, it appears larger than life. Help your visitors and customers to know more about you, what you do, and why you do it. There'll be a lot of organic traffic flow on your website, bringing you amazing results and helping you create a revenue footprint for your offerings.

You can start by creating a free YouTube channel where you provide value visually; your videos can also be shared very easily.

One excellent way to make customers love you is by featuring those customers on your platform. When you start featuring your highly valued customers on your platform, it encourages them to shop more. You can use the 80/20 rule of thumb here. 80/20 is the relation between the number of customers and how much revenue they're bringing to you. It signifies that 20% of clients give you 80% of revenue. You can use that 20 %, make them give you testimonials, and feature them on your website and social media handles. Apart from credibility, another advantage that this move gives you is traffic. This is kind of a no-brainer, but let me point it out anyway, people will be even more interested in sharing your profile now that they are featured in it too. You will also gain a lot of traffic from unknown sources. These anonymous sources may be from different industries, different platforms, and individuals working around the clock to make things happen. In no time will your customer base grow widely and even reach a point you haven't even thought of.

Make your customer a hero

The kind of marketing I'm going to mention below is a plan that never backfires. There's no name for it, so let me just write it down in a sentence for you. Make your customer a hero. Making them a hero and showcasing their capabilities and how they have been helping your company could get them talking. Even the influencers will love to work with you as your popularity will help them market themselves. This will result in many fruitful sales and conversions, which will effectively increase the pipeline and provide the much-needed cash flow to your company. All you have to do is give back more than you receive. The more you give, the more you get. This is based on quid pro quo. In the legal sense, the quid pro quo is something that you get in return for giving something. So always remember, you should be giving more to receive more. Same in the case of marketing, if you want more engagement on your social media platforms, you have to do a lot of networking, a lot of commenting, and liking other pictures, and other channels that are growing, and trending. There are chances of you getting featured too if you continue using this master move.

Planning to be unique by pitching your company in a very different manner to your visitors on social media platforms can help you win your customers over. The more you start giving back, the more gateways open and possibilities increase. This can also lead to a similar result as a lead magnet where you'll be able to gather a lot of leads, which can be your potential customers in the coming days.

Let's check out the five ways we can create trust in the minds of a customer.

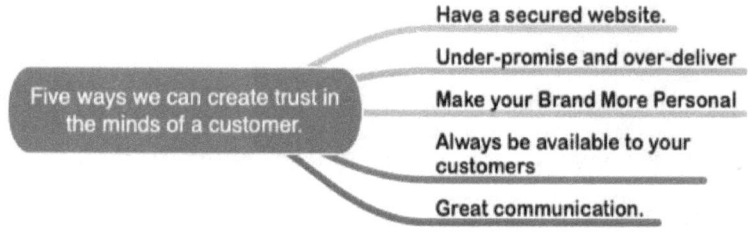

Gaining Trust Have a secured website.

Protecting your website with the help of SSL brings a lot of trusts when transacting on your website. It's similar to the feeling they feel when carrying a full amount of cash in a briefcase to your store. The customer should feel safe about their money; they should have significant trust in the brand. Having an SSL certificate will make your website secure and help you increase your rank on search engine platforms, which helps improve SEO rankings, as well.

Under-promise and over-deliver

Deliver more, promise less, or under-promise and over-deliver. You should always over-deliver in terms of what you're planning to give back to the customers. This makes them feel that their money is going into the right hands, more like, a good exchange of value. And when you successfully create a reputation for it, the customer won't mind paying more money for a better value the next time. This will help you bring the best out of your products/services, and if these offerings are long-lasting, make sure you inform to your customers. Bring the cost into the number of days, define them and give them a clear indication that this service or this product is limited to a certain amount of time. And that compared to other competitors, you're giving them much more.

Make your Brand More Personal

Bring out your personality, be friendly with your customers, and let them know who you are, not just what you provide. One way in which you can do this is by bringing the founder of the CEO into the picture. Show people that they're the face and the head of your company. Your brand automatically starts looking more human. We're all customers of something. Have you noticed a pattern, perhaps? Have you noticed why you're a loyal customer of a particular brand only and how they're similar to the other brands you love and are loyal to? The chances are that one of the reasons will be the persona all of them have created. When you give a brand a persona, it automatically starts looking more familiar and relatable.

Just think of Elon Musk. Any brand which Elon Musk touches becomes a huge, huge success. Be it, Tesla, be it Solar City, be it Boring Company, or be it SpaceX, every brand of that entrepreneur gets a prominent position in the market. Similarly, you need to bring that personal branding and create an impression of a more human nature than corporate. That will help you increase your business growth and ground you in a very systematic manner for future purposes.

Always be available to your customers

Provide them with the best possible customer service and give them a sense of availability in case anything happens. At some point, all of us feel the need to contact customer service. When they're approaching customer service, they should be very sure about how much information or feedback they would be getting in return to help out the customer who's facing any difficulty. Increase your availability to help out your customers in case anything goes wrong, and provide them with the best possible service so that you leave them assured and secured.

Great communication.

Releasing information on your website or even giving clear guidance to your customers regarding any possible situation, also if it's just you giving a few updates, it's necessary, it's essential. Customer feels like they're being considered, and that makes them feel special. You should even inform them in cases where you may have made a few mistakes. It's okay to be open about your mistakes. Everybody makes mistakes, and if nothing, this will only make you look more human. Your communication officer can decide on a fair communication strategy. Or, in case you don't have a communication officer, you can set a few principles that define some essential things that your customers must know.

Once you identify these things, they can be released with the help of the press or PR agencies, which will help you spread the information in various channels. This brings out a lot of credibilities and the form of vetting your customer's mindset and giving them a sense of trust. They are more than happy to know that a company is supporting them, always becoming proactive in providing solutions and guidance whenever it is needed. This will increase the loyalty in the minds of the customer, and increase your sales in a very efficient manner.

Remember, I spoke in brief about developing an online presence? It is essential because it gives a green signal to many other great tactics and strategies, ultimately making you the master of all things online. Yet, this is something that is conveniently ignored and neglected as somehow businesses don't find that important.

And that is what sets them apart from the master marketers, the big brands, and the A-listers. If you want to be in the big league, you need to start thinking like them.

Coming to the next topic, we'll be learning about how to create the best sales copy. People see so many ads in a day. Not just your competitors, but any brand in any industry can be your competitor in this circumstance. On top of this, it's a proven fact that users can't pay attention to an ad copy for more than 5-8 seconds. This means that you have only a matter of a few seconds to advertise your brand to them. In such a case, how will you stand out? This is why making a top-notch sales copy is essential. Just one headline should be enough to turn heads. In the next chapter, we're going to gauge the customer's minds; we're going to understand what copy stands out and what doesn't. We'll appreciate the difference between a good and bad copy, and much more. Let's get right into it.

Empowering Quote #12

Digital Marketing is a combination of art and science. First, understand the customers, develop strategies to reach them, and build a

relationship- Shubham Bapna

Chapter Twelve

Creating the Best SALES COPY!

Chapter 12 is all about writing the best sales copy. Sales copy is an essential tool for your business. Once you understand its power, you will know that it can determine whether your business succeeds or fails. This single skill is highly valued and still entirely unknown in the whole world. The world does not know its value or the skills that you need to harness for it, but now you will know. Once you're aware of the simple hacks I'll demonstrate in this chapter, you can implement them anywhere, anytime, at any place, and become a game-changer in the industry. You can use this skill to persuade anyone to take any action. This will undoubtedly lead you to great success in your business journey.

When handling business online, sales copy becomes a crucial tool since it's the only way we can convince our customers. We don't get to meet them or see them. But we can touch their hearts through our sales copy. Sales copy is not your regular stuff; it's something that can change your fortune forever. Get ready for this brilliant chapter because it's going to change everything you have ever known.

Types of Copywriting	Technical Copywriting
	Marketing Copywriting
	Brand Copywriting
	SEO-based Copywriting
	Direct Response Copywriting

Branches of Copywriting What is copywriting?

Copywriting is an art, the ability to use written words to persuade someone to take action. Copywriting can be diversified into five different types. Technical Copywriting, Marketing Copywriting, Brand Copywriting, SEO-based Copywriting, and Direct Response Copywriting. We'll be covering the marketing, branding and direct response copywriting here. These are the necessary levels of copywriting, which, once understood, can change your perspective and the way you persuade your customers. This time, you will learn how to encourage them to buy your offerings in the right direction. You can use them in your marketing campaigns, sales letters, or even when branding online. Such a level of copywriting would encourage your users to stay in touch with you and persuade them to do transactions that can lead to your financial wealth.

How do you write a good sales copy? Good sales copy consists of finding what's in the mind of the reader, understanding how they think, and how they react based on their value proposition, along with learning the art of persuasion, which will guarantee to turn mere visitors into loyal customers. What are you waiting for? This is a crucial chapter, so please read it thoroughly. One thing I want to clarify before starting is that copywriting cannot be learned in one or two days, or not even after getting done with this single book. If you want to learn to copywrite, you need to invest a lot of hours in planning, researching, unlearning, and learning before executing it. Knowledge is vast and unlimited; you learn something or the other every day. So if you've come into this thinking, it's some theory that can be learned in a matter of a few months and can be used for many more years to come, sorry to burst your bubble, but you're far from correct. In this era, nothing is permanent; being is always becoming. It's a long journey, but it is very much worth it!

Before we get started, I would like to give you a big congratulation for reaching this stage. Glad to see the dedication and commitment.

I can't wait to see how you incorporate my learnings into your business and become the success you have always wanted. Stay in touch with me on my website, unleash your business.online, or ShubhamBapna.com, I would love to solve your queries and discuss your success at length. You can also get in touch with me on my social media handles.

Now getting back to our book, let's start with understanding how sales copy really works, and then we can move on to the how-to of writing one. There's a massive structure that goes behind copywriting. Our ability to frame those into words in a manner that encourages the reader to go ahead and take action is what the objective of any copywriter is. As Mr. David Ogilvy, the father of modern copywriting said

80% of a copywriter's job is to write the perfect headline. You can take the same example in your personal life as well, what is the first thing you see when you read a newspaper? One sentence with bold fonts and italic design is enough to tell you if the column is worth reading or not. If the headline is compelling, only then will you take the effort of reading the news. It doesn't matter what kind of story it is. A catchy headline can turn your head and force you to read the content, and the best part is that people aren't even aware of its influence on their decision. That's the power of words. That's the power of copywriting.

Everything you see around you is the power of a copywriter, writing those sales copies that force you to take up action. Even if you don't want the product, you end up buying it, and to be honest, you're quite happy with it. The power of a single copy is such that it makes you feel like your life will be incomplete without the product's presence in it. Look around you. Every only thing that you've ever wanted is part of the structure of copywriting. I know you're wondering why I'm repeating the word copywriting again and again. Let me take you through the basics. What are the power words? Is there a formula? Where can I find the best copies in the world?

Let's start with the basics. So, copywriting is a simple arrangement of enticing words. With the right copy, you have the power to convince your customer to get whatever you want. And when you get such skills, you need to make sure that you meticulously use them, and take advantage, but don't be a freaking Thanos. You see so many ads in one day, but what makes some stick in your head? One of the differences can be the language or the tone of the copy. One may be catchy, while others are just informational. One may be information, while others are catchy. See, the context is not essential. What's important is that you stand out. Next time you see any ad or even read a news headline, look at it twice and figure out why this, out of all, made you turn your head. What were the terms of the power words that caught your attention? Next time, make a note or an online document, where you can store all these words, lines, whatever in that ad that caught your attention. This can be your cheat sheet. You can use this cheat sheet whenever you plan to run your ads or make a sales copy or even suggest to some friends.

Let's begin with the different ways and formulas that make

the copy the best copy.

- Before and After Bridge. Here's how it goes. Before, the world before you came to the rescue, after, how it could be after you came and solved it. The bridge is how you can reach there. This is the most classic one.

Also, the chances are that you're losing out on many sales right now. If you were on Suprcrowd, our people can market on your behalf and increase your revenue online. Register now at suprcrowd.in.

This, my friends, was the purest example of how you can create a bridge, a swipe copy, or even a file where I can share my words, my ideas in a simple context and encourage and persuade people to click on the link so that they can go towards suprcrowd.in. This was the number one way how I can simply create a copywriting formula.

PAS - Problem, agitate, and solve. You have to identify a problem, agitate the problem, and then solve the problem. First, focus on the issue that will get created if a person does not have what you offer. Then, agitate the problem, exaggerate and show them that this is a problem they've been facing for ages, and you might just have the right solution. Now, introduce the resolution.

- The Four Cs - Clear, Concise, Compelling, and Credible. By following this formula, you can always show your users that they need to be very clear.

Let's retake an example of Suprcrowd. First, I'll start by stating it in a simple sentence: it is An Automated Affiliate Platform, that's clear to you. A play of words that makes the user realize that you're different from others. Eg. You can list your business on this platform; You can get a hold of customer data.

Then comes compelling – You can get all of the above for free. (We all love the word Free, don't we?)

And now, credible. – More than 1000 businesses have put their trust in us.

This is one of the ways you can frame a copy in a way that informs the users about your product and also tells them what they will get from this.

Features, Advantages, and Benefits. I can use the FAB formula to show the features of this product, the many advantages over other brands, and the benefits of how it's going to make sense to any person who uses such a platform or a service.

- Four U's formula. Being Useful to the reader, creating a sense of Urgency, being Ultra-specific, and lastly, telling how it's Unique or what is unique in it.

- AIDA - Attention, Interest, Desire, Action. You need to

grasp the attention of the reader. Then, you need to create interest by providing them with something that excites them and forces them to read the copy. You can then create a desire out of it by giving some idea or some credibility about how this thing is going to work for them. Lastly, the Call to Action will be you asking them to register, pay, or purchase your products and services.

- Covering the primary objections. In point number seven, we are covering harmful codes. Here, I can show that I don't believe, I don't think that it works. I don't think that it costs so much money, or I don't think it will be helpful. Don't be shocked. The idea behind this is to grasp people's attention by starting the copy with something negative. People love reading negative stuff. Your headline or the opening line can start with something negative, and by the end, you can provide a solution i.e., your product and its features. Cliff-hangers. Now, this is interesting as it's related to psychology. Cliff-hanger is when you give them a hook. A hook can be in the form of a story that has become so sensational that it needs to be read by people, and they can't afford to miss it. If I'm able to create such a cliffhanger or a hook in the minds of the reader, they are going to click on the link without thinking twice.

- The Reader's Digest Formula. "Here are some fun facts you

didn't know about..."

Starting a headline with an adjective always gives you an advantage, they arouse curiosity. I came across this formula on buffer.com. I could see the difference after incorporating the same into my sales copies. Their article even contained short terms that can be used as follows: alteration, facts, a forest, opinions, repetition, examples, statistics, and trees. Mr. Carroll showed in such a creative way how we can fit the whole part of a forest in a blog post or a landing page or even on our social media. We need to use a few of the terms listed in a forest signal acronym according to our wants.

Give them three reasons why they should be choosing you.

The three ideas or the three questions could be –

- *Why are you the best?*

- *Why they should believe in you*

- *Why they should buy from you*

A single copy should contain the answer to these three questions.

- Using the ACCA formula. Creating awareness gives them Comprehension of how the solution could help them, providing them a Conviction or a desire by creating excitement in the answer you're offering. Then, action, which is the call to action that you provide at the end of every copy.

I've taken this from copyblogger.com. Their founder, Sonia, is fantastic in her work; what makes her so unique is that she uncovers the facts and provides you with the real story of how a good copy should be. We're talking about the 1, 2, 3, and 4 formula for possessive text. The number one could be - What have I got for you? Number two is - What is it going to do for you? Number three - Who am I? Number four - What is it that you need to do next? Providing things with a twist and following it up with a call to action at the end encourages them to click and go forward with your copy.

Brian Lark is the founder of CopyBlogger. One of the most potent websites ranked by many newspapers such as The Guardian, the Advertising Age, etc. This company has emerged as the most influential blog in terms of copywriting. And a lot of accolades go to the founder, Mr. Brian Lark.

We are creating a series of persuasive words. Series? How do we adjust so many persuasive words in one copy? Will it become overwhelming, or will it create a high pitch?

Suprcrowd is the best idea I've ever heard of in the last ten years of my tenure!

Isn't this statement compelling enough for you to click on

it? I've made use of not one, but many persuasive words here, and it seems to be working, isn't it?

- The Approach Formula. The Approach formula is more about how I can arrive at the problem. Show them the question, and propose a solution. Begin with a problem and then assure and reassure the readers that this is going to be an excellent solution for them. I can orchestrate some opportunities and ask them for the order by using the call to action technique.

The Six Plus One model. The six-plus model is from Mr. Danny Inny's Smashing Magazine. This formula includes - Context, Attention, Desire, the Gap, the Solution, the Call to Action, and showing the credibility. How can I use all of these and still manage to keep the copy small and effective? Example time. Suprcrowd is a widely used Automated Affiliate Platform (context), where entrepreneurs like you exhibit their products (Attention) and create demand for their offerings (Desire). This solution is free, to begin with, register now. A marketplace trusted by a thousand-plus businesses.

Here, I've covered all the points from the six plus one model, giving them an idea of how they can use and benefit by only going ahead and registering with Suprcrowd.

After presenting so many examples, I feel so empowered and happy to realize that these are going to change your fortunes, and your life, and increase your business' growth in a way you have always wanted. Here comes the last point—the Upwards Formula by Michael Fortin. Upwards means a universal picture, words, or relatable descriptive sentences. Something like - The whole world is using Suprcrowd for increasing their business. What's stopping you? Give them a universe. Make it relatable. This makes an impact on how they are being slowed down by something that they have not thought would be useful for them. So, go ahead and register for Suprcrowd, it's something that I would be using.

Okay, I am providing a bonus point. Here is a chance for creating an OATH formula, which is - Providing an Objective, creating an Answer, giving them a Thought, and showing them a Hurting sentence. But here, what do I cover from the OATH formula?

Do you know that your business is falling? And the only way to make it grow again is by registering with Suprcrowd. Do you want to miss them?

This eye-catchy yet straightforward copy grabs the attention of the user in a second. And now you can use it too!

Let me share a few tips and techniques on how you can become good at copywriting before ending this chapter. For this, I would like to give you a website. This website is called swipe.co. Swipe.co is a website where you can find bundles and bundles of different types of copies that are used all around the world. These can range from eCommerce companies, testing ads, split tests, banner ads, SaaS ads, or even display ads. They also provide examples of the old ads that used to be printed in old classic newspapers and magazines. Nowadays, since everything is online, we don't see much of such creative ads in the paper anymore. But you can find them on this website and make the most of it. You will also have an idea of what the swipe story or the files from the copies look like today.

Imagine if you were helping out a businessperson in solving their copywriting or in merely directing them to the right type of words or letters they should use on their website.

Imagine they're earning around $100,000 from that website, and now, with the help of the right copy, you're able to increase the sales from a hundred thousand dollars to $200,000. So that's a 100% increase, without spending even one buck on ads. I mean, the extra amount. Or without spending anything on adding new features. Or without going for an additional ad budget. Now you're able to increase their sales by optimizing the words and expanding the use of different formulas in the copywriting techniques. Imagine the kind of money that you could charge for this.

Even a 10% increase means you would earn $10,000 from just increasing and improving your copywriting. Imagine how powerful this industry is, but still, no one even talks about this. Everyone is talking about becoming a doctor, an engineer, an accountant, or also becoming a digital marketer. But let me give you an important fact. If you want to be successful in business, you need to have reasonable control and a great skill set on how copywriting works. That type of copy should be used, which is filled with powerful words that help generate sales, what type of terms could lead to results, and which ones could break down your purchases to multi-low levels. Don't make the mistake of underestimating this.

Use this technique wherever you can. With the help of so many tools that I have provided, you can get the correct version, and the right points to come ahead so that you can create a sense of Urgency, and uniqueness, be ultra-specific, provide a proper call to action and answer the questions.

If your customers have any requirements, leverage a possible story that can become your object and help you drive through the pathway of the copywriting technique. Do not use passive voice, but you can use something which is in the present, something which relates to something that has happened, and also makes an irresistible offer that the reader can never ignore. We have covered this part in the previous chapter, using a proper funnel technique, and along with copywriting, we can make a perfect combination.

Always use the power of testimonials, and with testimonial techniques, you can create urgency and give them a proper call to action. With an appropriate call to action, you can be rest assured that they will be clicking on the link, going ahead with a sale, or even registering for something that you want them to.

Now, heading to the next topic. The next question is all about automating your business process and how to do that in a perfectly structured manner.

Going ahead with chapter 13

Let me quickly summarize all that we've learned throughout till now since we're slowly reached the end. We started with unlearning, changing our mindset, and being open to new ideas. In my opinion, one of the essential things to do without grasping all the other knowledge that I've shared in other chapters is going to be challenging. As and when you change your mindset, you start seeing and understanding the possibilities around you. Analyzing the business, building your online presence by dedicating an email list, mastering the SEO, being present all over the Internet, adapting to new forums, making a good website, and developing a personal brand. Chapter Five was about creating a business story. Chapter Six was about identifying the right strategies. Chapter Seven was about the little-known growth hacks and techniques that I hope helped all of you. Chapter Eight was about spying on your competitors and finding out what the hell they're doing, and how are they doing it. Episode nine was about creating a proper sales funnel. Chapter 10 was about promotional offers that cannot be ignored. Chapter 11 was about how to win clients before even selling to them. Chapter 12 was about creating the best sales copy. Now when I combine all of these, I conclude. I come to a chapter, which is Automation.

Ever wanted a machine that works on its own, day and night, without you ever having to intervene to check on it? A machine that generates money for you daily. What if I tell you, today, you can create it? Remember, all the applications I spoke about and the right tools used correctly can automate your whole business online.

I think this is, by far, the most important chapter. Every established business has been using this process. Now, these are available to everyone out there who plans on growing their business online. With the help of online tools, it is now possible to connect all of them in a very systematic manner. I'll be sharing all the details with you. Right from –

- *Why do you need it what is its purpose?*

- *How can you do it?*

- *What are the possibilities?*

- *How much does it cost?*

- *And can you do it on your own?*

- Do you require a technical person to help you out in setting up all these things?

The answer is, let's find out.

Empowering Quote #13

The most important success secret for a Successful Online Business, is to use analytical tools properly- Shubham Bapna.

Chapter Thirteen

Automating the process

Over the last few chapters, we have understood that by using Unleash your Business Online system, you will be able to capture the true essence of automating your business and taking it to another level. Now, let me show you the different tools you can use in your business. By combining all of the lessons taught till now, you will be able to form a proper funnel that functions on a full automation basis. But first, let me understand from your perspective, why would you want to automate the whole process? If the answer is, you want to scale your business or want freedom from the old-fashioned, manual way of processing things, we've got you covered!

Why do we want freedom in our lives? Wasn't that one of the reasons for being an entrepreneur in the first place, too? We love to serve people, and we want to continue doing that, but without being bound by time, right? What if I say it is achievable?

With so many methods out there, it is possible to automate your business on a digital front. Using the powerful tools, which I'll show you, can help you connect with all the

applications you use that may be functioning in a different space, and keep them aligned. An automation process can help you keep your business upfront and generate a tremendous amount of revenue; day and night, it can work for you like your oldest salesperson.

Imagine hiring a robot that works every day, 24x7, for you. This robot is the same, only that it is based on a digital application. And the best part is that this robot doesn't cost you a bank, unlike the very much physical robot. Let me guide you on how you can digitize your business and automate the whole process.

Automating the whole process (part one)

In Part One, I'll share a few different ideas that will help you set a thought process and lead you in the direction of the kind of automation I'll talk about. Let's assume that you've already established a business online, gained customers, and are now planning on sending them automated emails to continue the interactions. What do you do? You enroll with an autoresponder.

I hope you remembered and said this out aloud on your own. If you remember, you'll know that autoresponder is an email marketing software. Have you ever come across emails like "thank you for shopping with us" or "thank you for registering with us"? Those are automated responses that companies send every time they see your activity on their website. You can achieve this either by hiring a person who can always keep track of your customer's actions and keep sending them emails. Or by merely installing an autoresponder, which does not even cost that much. Customers will think of this as a considerate move and will like the efforts you're putting behind the scenes to make this happen. But the fact remains that it is, indeed, an automated email.

You can even customize the emails by setting the first name as a dynamic field. This dynamic field will change according to the receiver's name, which means that if I get an email, it will start with something like - Hi Shubham or Dear Shubham and vice versa for others. Isn't this amazing? Having this simple process can help you build trust and credibility and loyalty in your customers' minds.

Nowadays, having an autoresponder has become more of a compulsion. You see, customers, by now, are so used to receiving such emails from companies that they start relating this to having a legit company. If a customer seems to have any doubt, they can simply respond to your automated mail, and then your customer service can take the conversation ahead from there. This is a straightforward tool and a pretty small step for your company, which will lead to remarkable customer service growth compared to your previously used non-automated responses.

I would like to share a few personal experiences of mine so that you can grasp the concepts better. As I mentioned before, when you come to visit my website, you are greeted with a form. When you click on that link, it goes to lead pages. First pages, as I mentioned in my previous session, is a tool that helps you build websites and landing pages that are highly convertible. You can find a small landing page with a photograph of my book, and inside it, you can find information about what this book can offer you.

Along with that, if you click the link, you will be able to download the first chapter of this book. After this whole process, we head onto the email. I have connected it to MailChimp. MailChimp is another email marketing software that is free to use for our 1st 2000 subscribers. If you're starting and are thinking of getting email marketing software, I highly recommend MailChimp. It's incredibly reasonable and, as mentioned, even free for a while, which helps you cut down costs in the beginning and serves the purpose of building a great email list.

Since I have integrated MailChimp, all the emails are collected and sent to the MailChimp database in my account. All my subscribers are added up there. If you're familiar with subscriptions, you'll know that you have to fill up a form with your name, last name, email id, and probably a mobile number. Behind the scenes in my database, your information directly adds up to your full name, and within a second, you get an email from me with which you can download the free PDF copy. The system is super-fast, by the way, and it makes you look professional too. Earning trust on a digital front is very important since the customers haven't had direct contact with you or know you directly.

By providing a free lead magnet in the form of the first chapter, I'm able to get information in return. And we all know in today's times, information is the most critical asset. Esp. The customer's information. With a well-built email list, I can market all the services I provide, upsell them, and build my sales funnel in a very structured manner.

I've compiled all the content in my book in a systematic manner. Once you start applying them in your or your client's business, you can unleash the business online. In just 15 steps, you will be able to capture the revenues that you or your clients have been waiting for.

They are now coming to the next step that I mentioned while talking about my landing page. Continue from there; once they click "Submit" on the form on which they've given their contact details to get a free copy, they're redirected to another page where they can register and get a discovery session with me.

With the discovery session, they will be able to talk with me for 15 minutes or so, and we can discuss all the business strategies that can help their business grow online. This is a free discovery session that I provide along with a free copy of my book. This way, I can connect with the interested person, and the chances of them buying my book will rise too.

What do I get from that? By integrating this single process of managing my calendar with the help of a tool called Calendly. I have purchased the premium subscription to Calendly, as I was so impressed by it. It helps me collect payments while booking any session, or even get my calendar aligned so that people can book directly from that application, and I can get on calls with my prospective clients. With this feature, I can simplify the whole process rather than calling them up and checking my calendar each day.

This works like an assistant, the only difference being this is extremely cost-effective. If you're not in the position to hire an assistant or just don't want to, this tool will help a lot. By not having an assistant, I can pretty much make sure that all the calls that were booked by people are highly qualified. When the user goes through all these steps before coming to my website, they voluntarily give in their details. Only then can they download the copy and then be redirected to another website where they can book a session with me; only a person interested in doing this will go through the whole process. This way, I can make sure that the leads are qualified enough to talk and give my precious 15 minutes. In these fast-paced times, automation is a must, almost compulsory.

Let me take you to the second part,

where I will show you some excellent examples of how I've been using different tools and making my business automated and much more real in the advanced stage. Since I also deal with online courses, I use Graphy. The two leading or big platforms for listing are Teachable and Graphy. They provide you with excellent learning management systems and tools with which you can host your courses, charge your customers, and a host of different features. They can help you out in expanding your coaching or online learning business. Since I've had my few online courses on the Graphy platform, if you would ever like to visit them, you can simply go to www.grandlaunch.co.

When you go on this website, you will be able to find different courses already live and have been used by so many people to learn, understand and implement the knowledge I've imparted into their businesses. They are more significant parts of my exponential online business Mastermind, the group that I've repeatedly been mentioning in my whole book, where this network of people comes together and helps each other out. I extend my hand to invite you to join this Mastermind group and make your presence felt.

Now, coming back to my example, while signing up for an online course, you might have to pay for a few courses while a few are for free. Let's assume you go for a paid course. If you're in India, you will be taken to a payment gateway known as Razorpay. I have connected to Razorpay with the help of a webhook. I'll be telling more about the webhook in the later part, but just know that this tool has even been connected with my Pabbly Connect API system. Pabbly Connect helps me connect webhooks in a manner that can collect information as well as post information. If I'm collecting some information from the webhook by Pabbly Connect into Razorpay, I can find out if there has been any payment made on Razorpay.

If yes, then it will automatically create an account on Graphy and send an email directly to the Registered User about their enrolment through an autoresponder. Do you see how all of these are linked with each other? I've connected five different tools that automate the whole journey without me having to intervene even once. It's helpful for both me as well as the customer since the whole process is so quick and seamless. The more ease I provide to the user, the more likely they are to stay loyal to me and, in turn, grow my business. You can have multiple steps, multiple applications, and multiple triggers that will work together for you behind the scenes to build your business.

Some may find Pabbly Connect costly, and if so, you can go for other platforms like QuickWork, or Pabbly. Pabbly and QuickWork are new in this industry and offer better deals. They offer lifetime deals, which can help you ease the whole process while restraining the costs that have been added to your monthly budgets. Once you know that you have the right amount of revenue or cash flow coming into your business, you can go for such advanced tools and applications.

If you ever want some help in setting up all these things, you can join my Facebook group. My fellow members from the group and I will help you with recommendations and any of your doubts. You can find the link on my website, unleash your business.online.

Part Three is about the tools that I've been using to automate the whole process of my business strategies. Pabbly Connect is the most widely used tool in terms of business automation in the online space. With Pabbly Connect, I'm able to connect with many applications that can work together. I can try, test them out, and then make them live.

With such a tool, I'm able to see the whole process and make sure there are no bugs that will cause me any problems when I'm going ahead. In Pabbly Connect, multiple tools and plans go into place. Some plans are very advanced; if I have several tasks lined up when my business is big enough, it will make sense for me to go to Pabbly Connect professional or business plans.

You can get started with Pabbly Connect for free. Pabbly is a relatively new tool that I have purchased as a lifetime deal. With a lifetime deal, I'm able to connect, make different tasks, and collect different applications in a simplified manner. Remember I mentioned Webhook? So what is that? Webhook has gained quite a good reputation in the last few years. Webhook is a URL that helps you connect and post information. Such a URL is adjusted in different applications, so when any transaction or a trigger of any situation takes place, the information is collected from that trigger point and is posted to wherever you would need it.

Let's take an example of how I was collecting information from my webhook. When there was a payment trigger on my Razorpay account, I call out the payments to be checked by my Razorpay account. If the payments were right, then every post something and the book would collect that and send that to my Graphy account. Graphy will then check all that data and see if the payment has been successfully made. It would enroll the user directly into the account, send them an email, and fire up my autoresponder. My autoresponder will send them an email and add them to my sequence. With a sequence, I can send you emails daily to stay connected with my customers. Such emails are beneficial and can help you increase your business revenues with the help of simple tools. These simple tools help you connect with different applications and make sure that your business processes are very much streamlined, automated, and ready to be scaled up. If you ever plan to scale your business, this is a highly recommended chapter that will guarantee to help you with all your doubts. But please do try it out. You will be able to understand if you keep trying out different applications and exploring your creativity.

You can also send your customers an SMS or a thank you call by merely setting that up in the automation stage. After setting that up in the automation stage, your users will get both SMS as well as an auto-email once they enroll. If you want to go for a more advanced stage, you can even record a small message that can be played while calling them up on an IVR system.

By setting up this IVR system, you're calling them up and giving them information about how you plan to go ahead, and how you're planning to change their life beautifully. Imagine the kind of connectivity and loyalty it would generate for your customers when they know that you care for them. When you're calling them and assuring them about their pain points, they instantly start liking and trusting you. This can lead to a long-term relationship.

Every business wants to be able to connect with its customers, and these relationships especially come to your advantage when you're planning to launch new products. When you have a good database of users, customers, and a good email list, you can send emails, create hype, and increase the chances of sales by adding all these things to your sales funnel. Who wouldn't want that? Ensure that you're following all these steps, increasing your email list, and adding them to your sequencing platform as it will help you massively in the future. Let these tools work for you day and night to make money even while you sleep. This is the process with which digital marketers and big businesses are earning and scaling their business to multi seven or eight-figure platforms.

You can do this too. You don't need to have a budget of millions of dollars; you can do this with a few hundred of dollars too. Go ahead and try all these tools out because only then will you be able to understand how things work and how you can apply them to your business. You can have multiple tools connected that are seamlessly working together to make your business secure and reduce your burden in terms of cost, as well as reduce the time that you spend doing all these mundane tasks. These tasks are something that we do regularly, but if there is a tool out there that can help you get out of this pattern and make life easier, why not take it up and use that time for something more substantial? Also, time and again, refer to the cheat sheet that I'll be providing you at the back of the chapter. It will help you connect with different types of tools and automation funnels. All these things can be downloaded from the link that I have provided at the end. Do check it out because it helps you stay connected with me and make sure that you get to download all these things.

And as for mastering these keys, it's simple. The best way to master them is by executing them. Go ahead, try them out, execute, and if your business is not set up yet, practice on your friends, clients, and family. This way, you can connect all the dots. You can get them structured in your head. You can put them on paper, make some mind maps, or use the powerful tools you have provided. With such tools, you will be able to prepare a proper funnel and proper digital automation.

Where can automation systems fail? If there are pros, there are cons as well. I have made a few mistakes along the way, too, in connecting these applications, etc. So this is very much possible.

Let's say I'm collecting some payments and I find a discount offer. Let's assume that this discount offer is only valid for a limited period. The problem arises when the time limit has reached its end, and the problem is that the whole payment structure stops all at once with it. When the payment structure is stopped, or the discount coupon expires, the link becomes invalid. And when the link is invalid, all the processes that occur after that go to waste could be a wrong message. It could be displayed in front of the consumer and is highly possible too, which can lead to a loss of sales in a business.

To avoid all these things, you must learn how first to operate these tools, see how it works for you, review all their policies and features in detail, and arrive at a decision. Some tools might work fine and impress you all over at the beginning and may just wear off after a while. Therefore, it is essential to use these tools in between regular intervals to see if it works well throughout or not. Check out the blog section on my website, where I've mentioned how you need to stay connected with all the automation tools.

Another way to master them is by building them for someone else. When you understand someone else's business, and planning, and give them the whole structure of how you can automate their digital business journey, you will gain maximum knowledge since everything is from scratch here. Not to mention, you will have to work from beginning to end without procrastinating since it's for someone else. You really can't go wrong with this method. When you start working on your business after this experience, you will be able to apply these tools in a much better way and even use your creativity to connect all these applications. Now that you know you won't make a mistake again.

Imagine doing it for your client; you have to deliver to them in a few days. This will force you to take the right kind of process with the least amount of integrations possible. When you have the least amount of integrations, then the whole journey, the cost that you spend on the automation part can be reduced a lot. The more reduction in cost, the more your business or your client's business will benefit.

You will be learning a lot of things in the next chapter, as in that, I will be talking about how you can unleash your business online so that all the above tools work in sync for it to happen. This will also lead to the 15th i.e., the last chapter, which is about scaling your business. We're giving you the extreme strategy of how you can showcase your business, showcase your products and services in full automation mode, sell them online day and night, and generate massive amounts of profit. I will also be discussing different platforms on which you can run ads and generate a high ROI in selling your offerings.

By investing in this book, you have made sure that you won't be the same you by the time you finish this book. When you complete this book, you will be enriched with so much knowledge that will help you structure your thoughts and give proper clarity on how to all these tools. It's almost time to take out all these strategies from the book and apply them in real life. Implement them, execute them, go through the trial and error, understand them, and make sure that you get them to work for you.

And as I said before, never leave a stage before providing a good CTA, so here it goes. In case you have any doubts, you can contact us on our Facebook group, where we will help you to get the best possible, unique strategies for you to unleash your business online. See you there!

Empowering Quote #14

The whole world cannot be your Customer. Once you define who your target customer is, you can go all in Shubham

Bapna

Chapter Fourteen

Unleashing your Business Online!

Congratulations! You've made it to the second last stage of unleashing your business online. How do you feel? You

must have understood the process and the systems to use by now. Maybe you weren't familiar with them earlier, and maybe that was one of the reasons your business was dropping. Don't worry, now with so much insight, all you have to do is start executing and applying this system to your business the correct way. This system will make your business grow day and night, even while you're sleeping. Ever heard of the two magical words, "Passive Income"? This system helps you increase and develop a source of passive income. The moment you digitize and automate your business process, you can rest assured that with the help of the tools that we'll be learning in this chapter, you will continue to scale up in a systematic manner that will help you grow your business in this digital age.

Today, I'll show you different ways to place your ads and increase your ROI. When you use paid ads, it becomes straightforward to target the right audience and reach them.

We'll be learning about the different ways, tools, and platforms with which we can place our ads efficiently. The different types of platforms that can be used for running your ads could be - Facebook, Google, Quora, LinkedIn, Tik Tok, or even YouTube. All these platforms provide you with high ROI in terms of the different products or services you plan on selling.

Let's assume your task is to sell my book. Where do you think my target audience hangs out the most? Since you're one of my targets, you tell me. Which apps do you frequent the most? Facebook? Instagram? Google? Twitter? LinkedIn? Quora? Perhaps, Amazon? You may not be familiar with Amazon ads, but they're useful, especially while launching this particular book. I know that this book will be beneficial for people interested in the same topic and are probably even searching for the keywords related to my book right now. Let's say they're typing keywords like, "Business," "How to take your business online," etc. on the platforms that I mentioned above, they'll see my paid ads, which will further lead them to my landing page and you know how it is from there.

The whole loop of exchanging my PDF for their information, adding them to my mail list, etc. will begin, and before they know it, they'll be in my funnel. I'll start collecting emails with the help of the system. Imagine the kind of collection of loyal customers, or even potential loyal customers I'll be able to get it. This is the power of running paid ads. You do not have to have a hefty budget to run ads. The value they add is so much more than the cost we incur.

I can run ads on specific platforms that reflect the kind of audience I'm looking for. There are tools available on these platforms, which help identify the content and the kind of audience that would be present when you're planning to launch your ads. You can do all of these even before you plan on spending a dime on the ads. You will be able to see the right amount of keyword cost, the number of people present in these categories, and different types of strategies that could be combined when you plan on selling to them.

Let's get started and understand how we can bring the whole structure into place. With a good sales funnel strategy, you need to define the pricing, promotion, tools, autoresponder, the digital business automation part, and experiment with paid ads. Paid ads can help you boost and scale your business as you have never imagined. Going from zero dollars to a million dollars is very much possible. Our goal is to reduce our costs while keeping our sales high, and don't worry; we can achieve that by merely understanding how paid ads work and what tools to use to make the most out of it. This book will be launched on all the platforms where I know my target audience will be, and my ads will be run on the same. Now since I don't know the kind of response I will be getting, I will launch and carefully observe the activities for a week. After a week, I will know the kind of ROI or response I'm getting, and I'll also be able to figure out which platforms were the most effective. Let's say I got the most response on Twitter; I will scale my ad spent on Twitter while reducing my costs on other platforms for the coming week. This budget will be set according to my business needs.

This budget will be reinvested in the whole process, and I will keep scaling this up until it pays off to the next level. A better plan to increase the ROI is by using your autoresponder.

- *But how can an autoresponder help me increase my ROI?*

- *How will the same amount spent by any reader on my book, justify the budget?*

- *Remember I mentioned about tripwire?*

If we take a broader concept view of what this book could be, it could be a tripwire! The pricing of a tripwire could be around $5 to $10 or Rs.300 to Rs.1000. If I'm pricing this book at $4.99, it means it's a tripwire. Imagine this to be a tripwire where people are paying you for your original idea. And then you can put them into the funnel, and send them emails about your new strategies, and your new tools, develop a relationship, then pitch them a new book or a course.

Imagine, by using a simple form of giving a tripwire, in this context, it's launching a book and getting paid for that will lead you to higher sales in terms of online courses or the next plan you have increasing your ROI. All these tools cost the right amount of subscription money. But when used properly, this can outrank you against your competitors. Your competitors will probably break their heads, trying to figure out what you're doing to increase your business to such an extent—and doing this on a very scalable model. This scalable model can be adapted to your business very efficiently. In case you face any problems, you know how to contact us. You can contact me personally on my email, too, which is listed on this book's website. You can find the link in the front or at the end.

I don't want to spoon-feed this whole concept and system to you. I believe you have understood how you can plan and build a whole strategy in a manner that can encourage creativity within you. With a lot of creative ideas, plan ads, create graphics, and run those ads, according to your business proposition. Remember, I briefly spoke about Amazon? My first choice of place for this book would be Amazon. Amazon allows me to run an ad on its platform. The book or the product being displayed can be made available to people who are searching for specific keywords that I've listed according to my book. Since this book is dependent on the number of sales happening on the ad front, I will also be sending the link to a lot of people there. The rise in sales will also count as organic traffic and will help people to search for my book, increasing the search volumes. When the search volumes increase, Amazon automatically recommends this to a lot of people.

The moment Amazon starts pushing this product to people, you will know that your book has become a success. Now, I'll be covering Facebook and Instagram together since both are connected. With Facebook's help, I can run ads and campaigns that will lead a book reader to my website. My website can simply collect the information, show them the benefits, and show them what they can earn out of this book. When the users know that the kind of outcome they would receive from this book is aligned with their needs, they will purchase this book. I can either lead them to Amazon or my website. I would prefer to buy from my website since I can cut down on the commission given to Amazon. Therefore, I'll redirect the audience to my website more as I need to plan and set up my book in a manner that increase the sales in a broader aspect. Rather than going to different places where the whole sales channel is distributed, I could just use two i.e., my website and Amazon.

Over some time, my book will be available on Flipkart, Snapdeal, Paytm, Barnes and Noble, and all the other publishing platforms in the world. I will also be launching an eBook, which will be available on Kindle and other platforms.

The gist is that the creation of an offering will help in

generating multiple streams of revenue from multiple channels, while the collection of all the revenues will be from one single place. This will be done with the help of a single tool, Notion Press, with which I was able to publish this book for free. Publishing this book only includes editing, transcribing, or even the time that I have spent on this book. My team and I invest in this book is the only cost that I can see coming up with the whole idea of unleash your business.online.

What if I plan on running my ads on Quora? Quora is a short form for questions and answers. It is a platform where millions of people can interact with each other by posting questions or answering questions in public. When a website receives a lot of traffic, they leverage its business model in such a way that it can display ads on it. Ads are a significant revenue source for many internet marketing companies, such as Amazon, Facebook, and Google. For some, their primary source of income can be ads. Ad revenue is so crucial for them that they even invest in highly robust tools to target the customers most efficiently.

If you feel all these systems and running ads, etc. is a big jargon, or you probably have a lot of other things to concentrate on, you can always contact my digital marketing agency, called Grand Launch. We can help you set all these things up so that you don't waste your time and money on trial and error and increase your returns while just focusing on the core product.

This way, we are running our ads. My agency is running my ads with the expertise of my fellow members and me. We can run our business and do all these things because of the digital tools available. Since we know and research all these tools day and night, we know which ones are the best, which led me to make this brilliant book. All you have to do is set up your business and focus on your core product; the rest all can be handled by a digital agency. By that, I, in no way, intend to say that all the other parts are non-core. They are also equally important, such as marketing. Without marketing, how do you expect your products to sell? With the help of all the tools that I've mentioned, you can strive for success. Daily, start implementing these small tools and techniques. Practice till you're perfect.

Your business can see new heights, and the kind of revenue you can generate is going to amaze you for life. If you ever find anything useful from this book, I'm sure you would be grateful if you could find me on social media, post a picture with your copy, and tag us. You can send me your pictures; I will repost them on my social media platforms by the name of 10X Shubham Bapna. This will make me happy because it would show me that my efforts in bringing this book together have made an impact on the world. It would be fantastic if you could send a video testimonial that I'll show my users and post on my landing page. It can also help you in branding your business and yourself on my social media platform.

Unleashing your business online is something anyone can do. Remember, you need to start with breaking the shackles, breaking the mindset. You can achieve anything as long as you put your mind, heart, and soul into it. Make a plan starting today. Explore all the tools I mentioned. The best part about going online is that there are almost always options available. If you find Marketing difficult, you can always hire experts just with a click of a button.

Businesses worldwide are facing so many difficulties in terms of digital marketing, online growth, reaching customers, increasing business, and branding during COVID. These problems are real-time problems. Now you have the power to solve all these problems for your business or clients. You could be a digital marketing company, a freelancer, or a business owner. You can use these strategies on your own, implement them, and see the results for yourself.

Now, let me take you through the marketing I'll be doing for a book to understand the kind of networks I'll be leveraging, the strategy I'll be following, and what will come next.

1. After I write this book, after proofreading and editing, I will send it to the publisher and publish it.

2. Next, I would buy a domain name in the name of this book, as you can see with unleash yourbusiness.online. This book is getting its branding, and its awareness.

3. I will install Google Analytics along with Facebook Pixel tools. With these two tools, I can track the visitors and target them with the help of Facebook ads, etc.

4. Now, I tell my development team at Grand Launch to build my website and make a great landing page. A landing page where visitors can visit and understand what this book is about.

After the website is made, I'll start making my social media accounts. In this case, I'll be using personal social media accounts on Facebook, Twitter, LinkedIn, Quora, Instagram, and YouTube medium to post information, graphics, and videos on this book. This the book will be spread across multiple channels, and the source would be led to my website.

5. Now, the funnel starts. When anyone visits my website, they can see a pop-up where they will be able to download a free copy, a free chapter of my book. When they download this chapter, their details will be captured. So I'm pretty sure that they are in my funnel.

6. Let's assume that someone doesn't give their details but wants to read more. They scroll down, see the details, see how the book is, see the reviews, and understand more about me and my book. They might also go to my social media channels, and find out where I've been mentioning the book.

7. When the testimonials start flowing. I can use them on my website, along with my social media platforms. With the help of SEO and a lot of paid marketing, I'll bring people on my website, get them to fill up the lead generation form, and then the whole funnel starts.

The next time they come to my website and are convinced to buy the book, they will directly go for a purchase, either from my website itself or from Amazon. I'll be allowing them to choose. Giving options to your customers make them comfortable because sometimes they are not convinced enough to buy too.

8. Let's assume the person goes to Amazon; what we can do is collect the information and redirect them. Once you collect the information via a contact form made from the ConvertKit email marketing software, you know which person has clicked on that and then add them back to your sequence. Once I add them to the sequence, I know who they are and if they have bought the book or not. If they bought the book, I could send them an autoresponder email to confirm they have bought the book. I can put a click here tab that redirects them to giving me reviews. And then, I can use a tagging system from the email marketing software to identify which user or which reader has bought the book.

Since I know how to segregate, I can find the right person and lead them to buy the book on my website. If people haven't bought my book, I can bring them back by sending emails and setting up auto-reminders. Once I bring them back to my website, I know that I have to give them something more. So I offer them some deals, coupons, and discount codes. They know that once they go through that system, the funnel, they would purchase it.

9. Let's say they happen to abandon the cart. I've also mentioned this, and if they are, I would be re-contacting them and sending them more discounts or deals that they cannot even ignore. This is concerning chapter 10, where I talked about promotional offers that cannot be ignored. You can see how powerful the system is.

I integrate the whole eCommerce platform on my website. I'm adding this WooCommerce plugin to my WordPress website of unleash your business online. I'm helping the user to do the transaction, let them buy, and then take them through the payment gateway. Here, I'm adding two payment gateways. One is PayPal; the one is RazorPay. Once the payment has been triggered, I use shiprocket. Ship rocket is a combined logistic platform providing its API for logistics and seamless support to get my products shipped to my customers. With this, my shipping has been integrated, and all the books will be collected and shipped by them. They will also help with packaging. Either way, I can hire another person to make this work seamlessly.

I'm aware that this book can be shipped to any part of the world. That's why I integrate Stripe. Stripe is another payment gateway that allows you to collect payments in any kind of currency. I'm enabling both Stripe and PayPal to collect payments in terms of dollars. The same method can be used to ship the products, such as this book, to international users. I can also use Amazon.com to get my books published and sent to millions of people in different countries. I can also use my eBook or the Kindle platform to enable users to read my book in an electronic format.

Nonetheless, I think people still hold onto hard copies and prefer them over eBooks. The feel is different; you can keep it in your sight, highlight, write notes, etc. on a physical book. While this argument can go on and on about how your customers like reading, let me point this out straight - Remember always to give a choice to customers. They are the kings, and your strategy is the queen. Once they combine, there's no stopping you from success.

What are you waiting for? Get started, sell your products and services, create your brand, grow your business, and make sure that you make a living and become financially independent way before any financial burden strikes you. Oh, also, shameless advertising, but go check out my YouTube channel. Subscribe, hit that like button on the videos you like, recommend what you want to see next by commenting, and hit that bell button so that you'll be notified every time I upload a new video. Make sure you get to see them beforehand. You can find me on all social media platforms, tweet about me on Twitter, or even catch up with me on tik tok. I'm present everywhere.

Like always, if you face any problems, you can always contact me on my Facebook group. The links are at the end; I'm also adding a QR code so you can directly scan them and reach my profile. Giving my customers the ease of understanding what I'm doing, and providing them with multiple opportunities to grow their business is what I love.

I appreciate the fact that you got this book and learned the chapters in detail. I'm sure this would have been of much value to you. Now, let me take you through the final chapter. I am scaling your business online.

Once you set up your business online, the next goal is to scale it. I'll provide as much information as possible, but if you want to learn it in-depth, you will have to wait for my next book. From my personal experiences to expertise, the book will have it all. If you're starting or have already started, you need to immediately start planning on how to scale this business to more than a million dollars. This is the time to get started. I'll be mentioning all the strategies that I've myself used and loved in the upcoming chapter. If you feel that you're qualified enough to start scaling your business online to multi-million dollars, go ahead and subscribe to my email list so you'll know when I release my new book. If you're reading this quite a while after 2020, the book would still be relevant. I assure you, you will be able to find "Scaling your business online" everywhere, in the bookstore, online store, or on the shelf.

This book, combined with my upcoming book, is going to make you a Business Owner no less than your dreams.

See you in the next chapter, future millionaire!

Empowering Quote #15

Take Action. You're just one step away from your Online Business growth- Shubham Bapna.

Chapter Fifteen

Scaling your Business!

Finally!

We are here in our 15th Chapter.

Scaling your Business Online

Now since you have covered all the elements carefully, we are going to understand how you can plan for Exponential growth Online!

Exponential growth comes from measuring the basics correctly. I will assume that you have taken care of all the strategies in order so that we can achieve the desired outcome.

We will be tracking every metric of growth that relates to our Business journey. When we plan to increase our Business prospects over the period, we can carefully increase our marketing budgets, which help us in improving the traffic to our page.

The improving traffic would be going through a similar funnel technique. This Funnel can also be converted into A/B testing. This refers to slight differences in the Funnel structure. This can be due to the change in power words, copy, or even

the colors. The response could be anything. What matters now is that the best way to find out the results is to test them. Testing of the different strategies will result in better business prospects.

- ☐ Track every metric

- ○ Tracking every metric will result in better marketing analysis.

- ☐ Other essential growth metrics are as follows:

- ○ Ecommerce growth — Where are most of my Visitors spending their money

- ○ Product assessment — Which products are my top sellers? Are there any opportunities to scale this up?

- ○ LTV: CAC (Lifetime Value: Cost per Acquisition) — Where are my customers coming from?

- ○ How much is the value per customer?

- • Using the Just in time inventory model to save too much capital being blocked in the Inventory. When you're scaling your Business and having a Product store, then inventory issues could arise.

  Use Dropshipping to grow faster

- ○ Dropshipping can become very useful if you get to hold a useful niche.

- Raise Funds from Investors if you feel your Business has high Potential. Look out for Maximum growth with the help of the Online Strategies mentioned in this book.

There will be revisions and updates in this book regularly. Also, make sure to join my Grand Launch Mastermind group. Link on my website. You will be able to learn and apply explosive Digital growth strategies meant for Business Owners to Increase their Sales and grow their Brand Online.

While going through the Book, you might have a lot of questions. Such questions can block your learning completely. But, do not worry. I have answered all these questions in the form of large blogs on my website. www.shubhambapna.com

A few of the questions are as follows

- How to take your business online?

☐ 5 Myths when taking your Business Online?

☐ Why should anyone start selling online?

☐ What are the best places to start selling products?

☐ Which are the best places to start selling services?

☐ How can a Business Owner move from an Offline to an Online model?

☐ Getting the pre-requisites ready for Online Business

- ☐ Should you have an in-house team or outsource it?

- ☐ Why going for a professional agency will help?

- ☐ How can a Large Business owner make use of it?

- ☐ How can you start selling your Products and Services in other countries?

- ☐ Why Digital medium is the best way to grow a business?

- ☐ How can one make use of the Digital Business Mastermind?

- How to use Digital Business Automation for Expanding Business?

- Will Entrepreneurs be able to scale their business using Growth Hacking Techniques?

- How will Business owners be able to use Digital techniques to Automate their Businesses?

- Is it possible for business owners to use Digital Marketing to grow their Brand Online?

- How will the Entrepreneurs be able to increase their Sales and Grow their Multifold?

- Is it possible to Run their Business from Anywhere & Anytime?

- How can Entrepreneurs use fresh Digital Strategies to grow

Exponentially online?

- How will Entrepreneurs be able to use Digital Marketing and Growth hacking to grow their Sales?

- How will the Entrepreneurs use Digital Business Automation tools to grow their businesses Exponentially?

☐ Will Entrepreneurs be able to redefine their Business Processes using Digital Growth Strategies?

☐ With the help of this system, How can Business Owners Increase their Sales?

☐ Will Businesses be able to Scale their Business using Digital Marketing and Funnels to increase their Conversion ratio?

☐ Business Owners will be able to Build powerful Digital assets that keep bringing them more business regularly.

☐ Have a system to track what your competitors are doing in business. And, Still outperform them.

☐ Why this Mastermind can be the best place to learn and grow your Offline Business, Online!

☐ How connecting with this Mastermind can help Entrepreneurs Unleash their Business Online!

☐ How Business Owners can 10X their business online?

Negative Questions

- ☐ These are the 10 Negative Victim Questions that my Customers are facing.

- Why can't I increase sales despite having a good online presence?

- Why can't I get online marketing to work for me?

- Why do I end up with shit leads?

- Why can't I get a stable ROI?

- Why is my Competitor killing me online?

- Why is online marketing so hard?

- Why can't I increase my sales online?

- Why is it so hard to build a strong online brand?

- Why are my sales not Increasing Despite Spending Money on Digital Marketing?

- Why can't I automate my Whole Digital Business Journey?

Empowering Questions

- What strategies can I use to Expand my Business Online?

- What can I do right now to Increase my Revenue Online?

- ☐ What can be done to end up with Quality Leads?

- ☐ What can be done to get an exponentially increasing ROI?

- [ ] What can I do to build a strong Brand Online?

- [ ] What steps should I take to Find a Good Digital Agency?

- [ ] What does it take to Build a Great Sales Funnel?

- [ ] What can I do to build high-converting websites?

- [ ] What tools can I use to automate my Entire Business?

- [ ] What can I do to Increase my Revenues Multi-Fold online?

Hope you have found this book useful. I will continue to bring you the best growth strategies so that you can Unleash Your Business Online.

Bonus worth Rs. 25,000

Unleash Your Business Online comes with an Online course and access can be taken from the official website.

Sign up and get access now!

https://grandlaunch.co

Quick Checklist

- [ ] Chapter 1: Changing the Mindset

- [ ] Chapter 2: Understanding the Possibilities

- [ ] Chapter 3: Analyzing your Business!

- [ ] Chapter 4: Getting your Online Presence ready

- [ ] Chapter 5: Creating your Business Story

- [ ] Chapter 6: Identifying the Right Strategies

- [ ] Chapter 7: Little known Growth Hacks?

- [ ] Chapter 8: Spying on your Competitors!

- [ ] Chapter 9: Creating your Sales funnel

- [ ] Chapter 10: Promotion Offers that can't be ignored

- [ ] Chapter 11: How to win Clients before selling them

- [ ] Chapter 12: Creating the Best SALES COPY!

- [ ] Chapter 13: Automating the process

- [ ] Chapter 14: Unleashing your Business Online!

- [ ] Chapter 15: Scaling your Business!

Power Words List

Here is a compilation of the power words that have been collected from Sumo.com

IMPATIENCE
Amp
Blast
Ignite
Jumpstart
Kickstart
Launch
Quick-start
Speedy
Supercharge
Turbo-charge
Smuggle

MEMORABILITY
Captivate
Genius
Memorable
Undeniable
Unforgettable
Unpopular
Impressive
Embarrassing

HAPPINESS
Heartwarming
Inspiring
Profound
Zen
Alive
Light
Healthy

PRESTIGE
Expensive
Glamorous
Luxurious

BEAUTY
Adorable
Awe-Inspiring
Beautiful
Breathtaking
Dazzling
Gorgeous
Stunning
Swoon
Swoon-worthy

LUST
Begging
Crave
Decadent
Delirious
Fantasy
Forbidden
Irresistible
Naked
Provocative
Seductive
Sexy
Sinful
Tantalizing
Satisfy

INDULGENCE
Guilt
Guilt-free
Indulgent
Obsessed
Ravenous
Lazy

EXCITEMENT
Bold
Exciting
Fascinating
Intriguing
Riveting
Tempting
Thrilling
Transform

NOVELTY
Challenge
Discover
Extraordinary
Hack
Latest
Life-changing
Magic
Miracle
New
Remarkable
Revolutionary
Sensational
Shocking
Spoiler
Startling
Suddenly
Surprising
Unexpected
Strange
Weird
Odd
Unusual

SIMPLICITY
Basic
Cheat-Sheet
Easy
Effortless
Ingredients
Minimalist
On-Demand
Painless
Rules
Savvy
Simple
Step-by-Step
Stupid-simple
Tricks
Tweaks

SADNESS
Alarming
Crushing
Dead
Deceptive
Devastating
Excruciating
Exposed
Heartbreaking
Sadly
Shaming
Suffer
Avoid
Demoralizing
Problem

SAVAGERY
Agonizing
Apocalypse
Armageddon
Battle
Corrupt
Crazy
Deadly
Disgusting
Fight
Frenzy
Hate
Insane
Lunatic
Menacing
Painful
Poison
Rowdy
Sabotaging
Savage
Sins
Struggle
Treacherous
Uncontrollable
Vicious
Violent
Weak
Wild
Dying
Horrifying
Attack
Traumatized
Insult
Horribly
Hell

https://sumo.com/stories/power-words - Part 1

COMPLETENESS	GREED	AUTHORITY	EXCLUSIVITY	PRIDE
Completely	Affordable	Absolute	Admit	Absurd
Copy	Bargain	All-Inclusive	Breaking	Achieve
Detailed	Barrage	Authentic	Confess	Awkward
Essential	Bonus	Authoritative	Confession	Blunder
Impenetrable	Budget	Authority	Divulge	Clueless
Meticulous	Cheap	Backed	Elite	Cringeworthy
Overcome	Convert	Bona fide	Emerging	Dumb
Painstaking	Double	Complete	First	Fail
Practical	Drive	Comprehensive	Hidden	Fail-Proof
Recreate	Forever	Conclusive	Insider	Failure
Replicate	Free	Definitive	Little-known	Faux Pas
Relentless	Immediately	Document	New	Fool
Ultimate	Increase	Expert	Popular	Foolish
Master	Instantly	Final	Priceless	Idiot
Perfect	Money	Formula	Rare	Lame
Super	Never	Genuine	Release	Last
Create	Now	Guaranteed	Reveal	Mediocre
Step-by-Step	Off-limits	Honest	Secret	Mistake
Best	Overnight	Iron-clad	Sly	Obvious
Truly	Profit	Legitimate	Sneak-Peek	Pitiful
Packed	Promote	Literally	Sneaky	Reject
Extremely	Sale	Official	Special	Rookie
Deep	Today	Powerful	Stealthy	Ruin
Better	Triple	Proven	Trend	Senseless
	Unlimited	Psychological	Truth	Shameful
GRAVITY	Envy	Reliable	Unadulterated	Silly
Gargantuan	Master	Report	Unconventional	Stupid
Gigantic	Lucrative	Research	Uncovered	Success
Huge	Steal	Results	Undercover	Threaten
Intense		Solution	Underused	Triggers
Massive	**HUMOR**	Strategy	Unique	Unknowingly
Gripping	Funniest	Studies	Unseen	Useless
Goddamn	Hilarious	Surefire	Untapped	Waste
Seriously	Laugh	Validate	Worst	
	Ridiculous	Masterclass		

https://sumo.com/stories/power-words - Part 2

Lean Canvas Model

Here is the Image of the Lean Canvas Model

Problem	Solution	Unique Value Proposition	Unfair Advantage	Customer Segments
Top 3 problems	Top 3 features	Single, clear, compelling message that states why you are different and worth buying	Can't be easily copied or bought	Target customers
	Key Metrics Key activities you measure		**Channels** Path to customers	

Cost Structure	Revenue Streams
Customer Acquisition Costs Distribution Costs Hosting People, etc.	Revenue Model Life Time Value Revenue Gross Margin

PRODUCT : MARKET

Lean Canvas Model- Copyright belongs to the owner.

Notes

www.ingramcontent.com/pod-product-compliance
Lightning Source LLC
Chambersburg PA
CBHW030623220526
45463CB00004B/1392